VENICE

TRAVEL GUIDE

2024/2025

A Guide to Gondolas, Off the Beaten Path, Hidden Gems, Savoring Traditional Dishes and Local Experiences

JANE M. BEASLEY

Copyright © 2024 by Jane M. Beasley

All rights reserved. No part of this book may be reproduced, distributed, or transmitted in any form or by any means, including photocopying, recording, or other electronic or mechanical methods, without the prior written permission of the publisher, except in the case of brief quotations embodied in critical reviews and specific other noncommercial uses permitted by copyright law

TABLE OF CONTENTS

INTRODUCTION 7
   Welcome to Venice 9
   The Allure of La Serenissima 11
   How to Use This Guide 13
   A Brief History of Venice 15

CHAPTER 1 18
PLANNING YOUR TRIP 18
   Best Time To Visit 18
   Navigating Venice: Understanding the City Layout 25
   Duration of your trip 29
   Venice on a budget 32
   Essential Travel Tips 36
   What to Pack for Venice 39
   Choosing the right tour package 41
   Entry and visa requirements 44

CHAPTER 2 48
GETTING TO VENICE 48
   Choosing the Best flights 48
   Venice airport: Arrival and Orientation 52
   Journey to Venice 54
   Train Options 56
   Bus Options 59
   Any other travel option for Venice 61

CHAPTER 2 64
GETTING AROUND VENICE 64
   Vaporetto: The Public Water Bus System 64
   Gondolas: A Traditional Ride 66

    Walking in Venice: Tips for Exploring on Foot...................68
    Venice by Bicycle: Exploring the Lido.............................. 70
    Water Taxis: Private and Group Services.........................72
    Navigating the Canals..74

CHAPTER 4...76
WHERE TO STAY..76
    Hotels..76
    Budget-Friendly Options... 79
    Luxury Stays in Venice..81
    Staying on the Islands: Murano, Burano, and Beyond.....84

CHAPTER 5...86
GUIDE TO VENICE'S NEIGHBORHOOD............................86
    San Marco..86
    Cannaregio...89
    Dorsoduro.. 91
    Castello.. 93
    Santa Croce... 95
    San Polo...97

CHAPTER 6...99
TOP ATTRACTIONS... 99
    St. Mark's Basilica..99
    Doge's Palace.. 102
    Rialto Bridge and Market...104
    Grand Canal: The Heart of Venice................................. 106
    Gallerie dell'Accademia...108
    Peggy Guggenheim Collection.. 110
    Teatro La Fenice...112
    Murano Glass Factories.. 114
    Torcello: Venice's Ancient Island.................................... 118

CHAPTER 7 120
HIDDEN GEMS AND OFF-THE-BEATEN-PATH EXPERIENCE 120
- Exploring the Secret Gardens of Venice 120
- Visiting the Libreria Acqua Alta 122
- Scuola Grande di San Rocco 124
- The Quiet Charm of Giudecca 126
- Discovering the Jewish Ghetto 128
- Venetian Mask Workshops 131

CHAPTER 8 133
CULTURAL EXPERIENCES 133
- The Venice Carnival: A World of Masks and Mystery 133
- Art and Architecture: From Byzantine to Baroque 136
- Music and Opera in Venice 138
- Venice's Festivals and Events 140
- Venice's Nightlife: Bars, Clubs, and Jazz Venues 142
- Venice's Artisan Crafts: Lace, Glass, and Masks 145

CHAPTER 9 147
DAY TRIPS FROM VENICE 147
- Visiting the Prosecco Wine Region 147
- A Day in Padua 149
- Exploring the Villas of the Brenta Canal 151
- The Charming Town of Treviso 153
- The Natural Beauty of the Po Delta 156

CHAPTER 10 159
VENETIAN CUISINE 159
- Traditional Venetian Dishes You Must Try 159
- Best Restaurants in Venice 162
- Wine Bars and Bacari: Venetian Tapas Culture 167

Venice's Food Markets: Rialto Market and More........... 170
Cooking Classes and Food Tours................................... 173
Vegetarian and Vegan Dining in Venice......................... 175

CHAPTER 11..178
VENICE WITH FAMILY...178
Family-Friendly Attractions...178
Activities for Kids in Venice... 180
Tips for Traveling with Children....................................... 183
Best Places to Eat with Kids.. 185

CHAPTER 12..187
PRACTICAL INFORMATION... 187
Currency And Payments.. 187
Language Tips for Travelers..190
Health and Safety in Venice.. 193
Emergency Contacts and Services................................. 196
Accessible Venice: Tips for Travelers with Disabilities... 199
Sustainable Travel in Venice... 202
CONCLUSION... 205
MAP.. 208

INTRODUCTION

Venice is a city like no other, with its winding canals, historic buildings, and charming bridges. It feels almost magical, as if it's taken straight from a fairy tale. The pastel-colored buildings reflect in the water, and the sound of gondolas gliding by adds to the city's enchanting atmosphere. Venice is not just a place to visit; it's an experience that captivates your senses and your heart.

My own journey to Venice was a serendipitous one. I wasn't usually the adventurous type. I preferred relaxing vacations with a good book on a quiet beach. But one rainy afternoon, as I was reading *The Merchant of Venice* in my school library, something changed. The book's vivid descriptions of Venice's canals and people sparked a curiosity within me that I couldn't ignore.

Driven by this newfound wanderlust, I dove into researching Venice. Online guides showed me beautiful photos, but they didn't capture the full essence of the city. So, I decided to take the plunge, booking a flight and a cozy hotel near St. Mark's Square.

When I arrived, the sight of Venice was like stepping into a dream. The city's unique architecture and charming canals were breathtaking. The air was filled with the smell of fresh bread, and the sound of gondolas added to the city's magical atmosphere.

During my stay, I explored Venice's narrow streets, marveled at its stunning buildings, and enjoyed a gondola ride through the canals. I visited the lively St. Mark's Square and discovered hidden courtyards and small, family-run restaurants with delicious seafood. I even saw a glass-blowing demonstration on Murano Island.

Sitting in a quiet café, watching Venice's beauty unfold, I felt incredibly grateful. What began as a simple curiosity had led me to an extraordinary adventure. It reminded me that sometimes the most amazing experiences start with the smallest sparks of curiosity.

In this book, you'll find everything you need to embrace the Venice experience. From exploring its iconic sights to discovering hidden gems, you'll learn how to make the most of your visit. This guide will help you navigate Venice's enchanting canals, savor its delicious food, and uncover the city's rich history and culture.

I invite you to dive into this book and let it be your companion as you explore Venice. Discover the magic of this extraordinary city and create your own unforgettable memories. Let your journey begin here.

Welcome to Venice

Welcome to Venice, a city that feels like stepping into a painting where every brushstroke tells a story of romance, history, and timeless beauty. The moment you arrive, you'll feel the magic of this floating city, where the streets are made of water and the buildings seem to rise straight from the lagoon. There's something almost surreal about Venice; it's a place that captures your imagination and never lets go.

As you make your way through the narrow alleys and across the charming bridges, you'll notice the way the light reflects off the canals, casting a golden hue over everything. The sound of water lapping against the ancient stone walls, the distant echo of a gondolier's song, and the scent of the sea in the air all create an atmosphere that is both peaceful and vibrant. It's a city where time seems to slow down, allowing you to fully immerse yourself in its unique charm.

Venice is not just a destination; it's an experience. Each of its six districts, or sestieri, offers a different perspective on the city's character. From the bustling heart of San Marco with its iconic landmarks like St. Mark's Basilica and the Doge's Palace, to the quieter, more residential areas like Cannaregio and Castello, Venice invites you to explore its many layers.

Every corner you turn reveals a new surprise, whether it's a hidden courtyard, a quaint café, or a view of the lagoon that takes your breath away.

There's something for everyone here, whether you're an art lover, a history buff, or simply someone who enjoys wandering without a plan. You can spend hours exploring the museums and galleries that house masterpieces from the Renaissance, or you can lose yourself in the maze of streets, discovering small shops selling handmade Venetian masks and delicate glass from Murano. And of course, no visit to Venice is complete without experiencing the joy of a gondola ride, gliding through the canals as you soak in the city's beauty from the water.

As you settle into the rhythm of Venice, you'll start to understand why so many people fall in love with this city. It's not just about the sights, though they are undoubtedly stunning; it's about the feeling Venice gives you, a sense of being somewhere truly special. This is a place where history comes alive, where every building has a story to tell, and where the simple act of wandering can lead to unforgettable moments.

So, take your time and let Venice reveal itself to you at its own pace. Allow yourself to get lost in its winding streets, to pause on a bridge and watch the gondolas pass below, to sit in a quiet square and listen to the sounds of the city. Venice is a place to be savored, one moment at a time. Welcome to a city like no other, where the past and present blend seamlessly together, creating a timeless beauty that will stay with you long after you've left its shores.

The Allure of La Serenissima

The allure of Venice, often called "La Serenissima," lies in its timeless elegance and undeniable charm. The name itself, meaning "The Most Serene," captures the essence of this city that has captivated travelers, artists, and dreamers for centuries. Venice is a place where history, art, and culture intertwine in a way that feels almost magical, creating an atmosphere that is both serene and captivating.

What makes Venice so special is the way it seems to float between reality and fantasy. The city is built on a series of small islands connected by canals and bridges, creating a landscape that is unlike anywhere else in the world. As you wander through its narrow alleys and along its winding canals, you'll feel as if you've stepped into a different time. The absence of cars and the gentle sound of water lapping against the buildings add to the sense of tranquility that defines Venice.

Venice has a unique way of drawing you in, making you want to explore every hidden corner and discover its secrets. The city's beauty is not just in its grand landmarks but also in the small, often overlooked details that make it so enchanting. The weathered facades of the buildings, the intricate patterns of the wrought-iron balconies, and the colorful reflections in the water all contribute to the city's allure.

One of the most captivating aspects of Venice is its ability to blend the old with the new. While the city is steeped in history, with its grand palaces and churches telling stories of a glorious past, it is also a living, breathing place where modern life continues to unfold. This juxtaposition creates a dynamic that keeps Venice vibrant and ever-changing, while still holding on to its timeless appeal.

Venice is also a city of art and culture. It has been a hub of creativity for centuries, inspiring countless artists, writers, and musicians. The city's rich artistic heritage is evident in its many museums, galleries, and theaters. Whether you're admiring the masterpieces in the Gallerie dell'Accademia, exploring the contemporary art at the Peggy Guggenheim Collection, or attending an opera at La Fenice, you'll find that Venice's cultural offerings are as diverse as they are impressive.

But the true allure of Venice goes beyond its physical beauty and cultural riches. It's the way the city makes you feel that leaves a lasting impression. There's a sense of romance and mystery here that is hard to put into words. It's in the way the light changes throughout the day, casting a golden glow over the city at sunset. It's in the quiet moments when you find yourself alone on a bridge, watching the gondolas glide by below. It's in the sense of discovery that comes with every turn of a corner, where you never know what hidden gem you might find next.

Venice invites you to slow down and savor each moment. It's a city that rewards those who take the time to explore its depths, to appreciate its beauty, and to lose themselves in its unique atmosphere. The allure of La Serenissima is not just in what you see, but in what you feel—the sense of connection to a place that is both timeless and ever-changing, serene and vibrant, ancient and alive.

How to Use This Guide

As you embark on your journey through Venice, this guide is here to help you make the most of your experience. It's designed to be your companion, offering insights, tips, and suggestions that will enhance your time in this beautiful city. Whether you're a first-time visitor or someone who has wandered Venice's canals before, this guide will provide you with the information you need to explore the city with confidence and ease.

This guide is organized to help you navigate Venice in a way that feels natural and enjoyable. It covers everything from the city's must-see sights to hidden gems that you might not find in a typical guidebook. The idea is to give you a well-rounded view of Venice, allowing you to experience both its iconic landmarks and its lesser-known treasures.

As you read through this guide, you'll find descriptions of the different areas of Venice, each with its own unique character and attractions. Whether you're interested in exploring the bustling heart of the city around St. Mark's Square, or you prefer to wander through the quieter, more residential neighborhoods, this guide will point you in the right direction. It's like having a local friend show you around, sharing their favorite spots and offering practical advice along the way.

One of the key things to remember while using this guide is that Venice is a city best explored at your own pace. The beauty of Venice lies in its details, and sometimes the most memorable moments happen when you least expect them. So, while this guide will give you plenty of ideas for things to see and do, don't feel like you have to follow a strict itinerary. Take your time, let your curiosity lead the way, and be open to the surprises that Venice has to offer.

This guide also includes practical information to make your trip smoother. You'll find tips on transportation, including how to get around the city by foot, boat, or even gondola. There are recommendations for dining, from casual eateries where you can grab a quick bite to more formal restaurants where you can enjoy a leisurely meal. And because Venice can be overwhelming with its wealth of art, history, and culture, this guide will help you prioritize what to see based on your interests and the time you have.

Throughout this guide, you'll also find suggestions for how to experience Venice in a way that's both authentic and respectful of the city's rich heritage. Venice is a city with deep cultural roots, and by following some simple tips, you can help preserve its beauty for future generations. This might include choosing less crowded times to visit popular sites, supporting local businesses, or exploring off the beaten path to discover a quieter side of the city.

Above all, this guide is here to help you create your own unique experience in Venice. It's meant to inspire you, to give you ideas, and to provide you with the tools you need to make the most of your time in this extraordinary city. Whether you're here for a day, a week, or longer, Venice has something special to offer every visitor, and this guide will help you uncover it. So, take it with you as you explore, let it guide you when you need it, and most importantly, enjoy every moment of your Venetian adventure.

A Brief History of Venice

Venice's history is as captivating as the city itself, a story of resilience, ambition, and creativity that spans over a thousand years. The city's beginnings date back to the early 5th century when people from the mainland fled to the marshy islands of the Venetian Lagoon to escape invasions by barbarian tribes. These early settlers built their homes on the small islands, gradually transforming the swampy terrain into the foundation of what would become one of the most powerful and unique cities in the world.

By the 9th century, Venice had established itself as an important center of trade. Its strategic location at the crossroads of Europe and the East allowed Venetian merchants to dominate the trade routes, bringing spices, silks, and other luxury goods from the East to Europe. This wealth fueled Venice's growth, and the city became a hub of commerce, culture, and art. The Venetian Republic, also known as La Serenissima, was officially established, and Venice began its rise as a maritime power.

Venice's golden age spanned from the 12th to the 15th centuries, a period when the city reached the height of its power and influence. The Venetian fleet was one of the strongest in the Mediterranean, and Venice's territories extended across the Adriatic Sea and beyond. During this time, the city's famous landmarks, such as St. Mark's Basilica, the Doge's Palace, and the Rialto Bridge, were constructed, showcasing the wealth and artistic prowess of the Republic.

Art and culture flourished in Venice, with the city becoming a center of the Renaissance. Venetian artists like Titian, Tintoretto, and Veronese produced masterpieces that are still celebrated today. The city's architecture, with its distinctive Gothic and Byzantine influences, reflected Venice's role as a melting pot of cultures. The canals, palaces, and churches that define Venice's landscape are testaments to this era of prosperity and artistic achievement.

However, Venice's fortunes began to decline in the late 16th century. The rise of new trade routes, particularly the discovery of the Americas, shifted the center of global trade away from the Mediterranean. Additionally, wars with the Ottoman Empire and other European powers weakened Venice's military and economic power. Despite these challenges, Venice remained a cultural beacon, continuing to produce art, music, and literature that captivated the world.

In 1797, Venice's long independence came to an end when Napoleon Bonaparte conquered the city, marking the fall of the Venetian Republic. Venice was subsequently handed over to the Austrian Empire, and later became part of the Kingdom of Italy in 1866. Despite these political changes, Venice retained its distinct identity and continued to be a symbol of beauty and history.

Throughout the 19th and 20th centuries, Venice transformed into a major tourist destination, drawing visitors from around the world who were enchanted by its canals, architecture, and rich history. Today, Venice faces challenges related to preservation, rising sea levels, and the impacts of tourism, but it remains a city of extraordinary allure.

Venice's history is a tale of transformation, resilience, and cultural richness. From its humble beginnings in the lagoon to its rise as a powerful maritime republic, and eventually to its status as a global icon, Venice has always been a city that captures the imagination. As you walk through its streets and float along its canals, you're not just exploring a city—you're stepping into a living history that continues to inspire and enchant.

CHAPTER 1.
PLANNING YOUR TRIP

Best Time To Visit

When it comes to deciding the best time to visit Venice, each season offers its own charm and unique experiences. Whether you prefer the warmth of the summer sun or the quiet beauty of winter, understanding what each season has to offer will help you plan a trip that matches your interests and travel goals.

Spring in Venice
Spring is a delightful time to visit Venice, with the city awakening from its winter slumber as flowers bloom and the days grow longer. The weather is mild, with temperatures ranging from the low 50s to the mid-60s Fahrenheit. The city feels fresh and vibrant, and the canals sparkle under the gentle sunlight. The crowds are smaller compared to the summer months, making it an ideal time for leisurely exploration.

In spring, the Venetian landscape comes alive with colorful gardens, and there's a sense of renewal in the air. Key attractions like St. Mark's Square and the Doge's Palace are less crowded, allowing you to appreciate their beauty without feeling rushed. The Venice Biennale, one of the world's most prestigious cultural events, often kicks off in late spring, drawing art enthusiasts from around the globe.

For practical tips, pack layers, as the weather can be unpredictable. A light jacket and comfortable walking shoes are essential. Be prepared for occasional showers, so an umbrella or a waterproof jacket is a good idea. Spring is a season of renewal and beauty, but the weather can still be cool, especially in the evenings.

Travel tips for spring include enjoying a gondola ride without the intense summer heat and exploring the city's quieter corners, such as the Castello district. You might also catch the Festa della Sensa in May, a traditional Venetian celebration that includes a symbolic marriage of the sea and a grand regatta.

Crowds in spring are moderate, and prices for accommodations are generally lower than in the peak summer months. It's a great time to experience Venice's famous sights without the throngs of tourists. If you prefer a more relaxed pace, spring is ideal. You can enjoy Venice's beauty without the hustle and bustle of high season.

Compared to other seasons, spring offers a perfect balance between pleasant weather and manageable crowds. It's a time when Venice is still relatively peaceful, making it a great choice for those who want to experience the city's charm without the intensity of summer.

Summer in Venice
Summer in Venice is both lively and intense. The city is bathed in warm sunlight, and the days are long and bright. Temperatures can soar into the 80s, and sometimes even higher, making it the warmest time of the year. The canals shimmer under the sun, and the city's vibrant energy is

palpable. This is peak tourist season, so Venice is bustling with visitors from around the world.

The landscape of Venice in summer is stunning, with the Grand Canal reflecting the bright blue sky, and the city's historic buildings standing in sharp contrast against the vibrant colors of the season. Summer is the time for outdoor activities, whether it's sipping an espresso in a sun-drenched piazza or taking a boat ride to the nearby islands of Murano and Burano.

For practical tips, pack light, breathable clothing, a hat, and plenty of sunscreen to protect yourself from the sun. Comfortable sandals or walking shoes are a must, as you'll likely be doing a lot of exploring on foot. While Venice's narrow streets provide some shade, it's important to stay hydrated and take breaks in the cool interiors of churches or museums.

Travel tips for summer include enjoying Venice's many outdoor festivals and events. The Festa del Redentore in July is a highlight, with its spectacular fireworks display over the lagoon. You can also take advantage of the long daylight hours to explore the city at your own pace. Just be prepared for larger crowds, especially around major attractions.

Crowds and costs peak in summer, so expect higher prices for accommodations and longer lines at popular sites. However, with some planning, you can still find quieter moments, such as an early morning stroll through the empty streets or a sunset boat ride along the Grand Canal. Summer is also the best time for those who enjoy the lively atmosphere of a bustling city.

Compared to other seasons, summer in Venice is all about vibrancy and energy. If you enjoy the buzz of a crowded city and don't mind the heat, summer is the perfect time to experience Venice's lively spirit. However, if you prefer a quieter, more relaxed visit, you might want to consider another season.

Autumn in Venice
Autumn brings a sense of calm and reflection to Venice. The summer crowds begin to disperse, and the city takes on a more relaxed pace. Temperatures cool down to a comfortable range, from the mid-50s to the low 70s Fahrenheit. The crisp air and soft, golden light create a magical atmosphere, and the city's historic architecture looks especially stunning against the backdrop of changing leaves.

Venice in autumn is a feast for the senses. The city's markets are filled with seasonal produce, and the restaurants start serving heartier dishes that reflect the flavors of the season. The calm waters of the lagoon mirror the warm hues of the autumn sky, making it a perfect time for photography and quiet contemplation. Key attractions are more accessible, allowing you to explore at a leisurely pace.

For practical tips, pack layers to adjust to the changing temperatures. A light sweater or jacket is recommended for the cooler evenings, and comfortable shoes are still a must for walking the city's many bridges and cobblestone streets.

Autumn is also a time when occasional rain showers might occur, so having an umbrella handy is wise.

Travel tips for autumn include visiting Venice's museums and galleries, which are less crowded at this time of year. The Venice International Film Festival, held in early September, is a major event that attracts film enthusiasts and celebrities. It's also a great time to take a day trip to the nearby vineyards of the Veneto region to enjoy the autumn harvest.

Crowds in autumn are thinner than in summer, and prices for accommodations begin to drop. This makes autumn an excellent time to experience Venice's culture and history without the rush of peak season. You can enjoy a more personal connection with the city, whether it's through a quiet walk along the canals or a peaceful gondola ride.

Compared to other seasons, autumn offers a perfect blend of mild weather, fewer tourists, and the opportunity to experience Venice in a more intimate way. It's an ideal time for those who appreciate art, culture, and a slower pace of travel.

Winter in Venice
Winter in Venice is a time of quiet beauty and reflection. The city is often enveloped in a soft mist that adds a mysterious, almost dreamlike quality to the landscape. Temperatures can range from the low 30s to the mid-40s Fahrenheit, and while it can be chilly, Venice rarely experiences snow. The streets are much quieter, and the city takes on a peaceful, almost serene atmosphere.

Venice in winter is a place of contrasts. The grandeur of the city's architecture stands out even more against the winter sky, and the canals, often veiled in fog, create an enchanting scene. It's a time when Venice feels like it belongs to the locals, and you can experience the city's authentic character away from the tourist crowds.

For practical tips, pack warm clothing, including a good coat, scarf, gloves, and waterproof boots. Venice's winter can be damp, so it's important to dress in layers to stay warm and comfortable. The city's indoor attractions, such as museums and churches, provide a welcome respite from the cold, so be sure to plan some indoor activities.

Travel tips for winter include visiting during the Venice Carnival, which usually takes place in February. This vibrant festival is one of the most famous events in the world, featuring elaborate masks, costumes, and parades. It's a magical time to be in Venice, but be sure to book your accommodations well in advance, as the city fills up quickly during the carnival.

Crowds in winter are minimal, except during the carnival season, and prices for accommodations are generally lower, making it an attractive time for budget-conscious travelers. You can enjoy a quieter, more introspective Venice, where you can linger over a coffee in a cozy café or explore the city's narrow streets without the usual hustle and bustle.

Compared to other seasons, winter in Venice is for those who appreciate tranquility and a more intimate experience of the city. It's a time to soak in the atmosphere, enjoy the beauty of Venice in its quieter moments, and perhaps see the city from a different perspective. While it may not be as warm as summer or as lively as spring, winter offers its own special charm.

Venice offers something unique in every season. Spring is perfect for those who want to experience the city in bloom with moderate crowds. Summer is vibrant and lively, ideal for those who enjoy the energy of peak season. Autumn provides a balance of mild weather and fewer tourists, making it a great time for cultural exploration. Winter offers tranquility and the chance to see Venice in a more intimate and peaceful light. Your choice of when to visit Venice will depend on what kind of experience you're looking for, but rest assured, each season has its own magic in this timeless city.

Navigating Venice: Understanding the City Layout

Navigating Venice is a unique experience, unlike any other city you may have visited. Venice is a city built on water, with canals serving as roads and boats replacing cars. The city's layout can be confusing at first, but with a bit of understanding, it becomes a place of endless discovery.

Venice is made up of 118 small islands connected by over 400 bridges, and it's divided into six main districts, known as "sestieri." These districts are Cannaregio, San Marco, Castello, Dorsoduro, San Polo, and Santa Croce. Each sestiere has its own distinct character and charm, offering something different for every visitor. Understanding these districts will help you get a better sense of where you are and what to explore.

San Marco is the heart of Venice, home to the famous St. Mark's Square, the Doge's Palace, and the Basilica di San Marco. This area is the most popular with tourists, so it can be crowded, but it's also where you'll find some of Venice's most iconic landmarks. The square is a great starting point for your exploration, as it's centrally located and gives you easy access to the rest of the city.

Cannaregio, located in the northern part of the city, is one of the most authentic Venetian neighborhoods. It's less crowded than San Marco and offers a glimpse into the everyday life of Venetians. This district is where you'll find the Jewish Ghetto, a historic area that's rich in culture and history. Cannaregio is also a great place to enjoy local restaurants and bars away from the tourist crowds.

Castello is the largest sestiere and stretches from the lively areas near St. Mark's Square to the quieter, more residential parts of Venice. The eastern part of Castello is home to the Biennale Gardens, where the Venice Biennale, an international art exhibition, is held. This district is perfect for those who want to explore both the bustling and peaceful sides of Venice.

Dorsoduro is a vibrant district known for its art and culture. It's home to the Peggy Guggenheim Collection, one of the most important museums of modern art in Italy, and the Accademia Gallery, which houses a collection of Venetian paintings. Dorsoduro is also where you'll find the lively Campo Santa Margherita, a square that's popular with students and locals, making it a great place to soak up the atmosphere.

San Polo and Santa Croce are located in the western part of Venice and are the city's oldest neighborhoods. San Polo is famous for the Rialto Market, where you can experience the bustling activity of a traditional Venetian market. The Rialto Bridge, one of Venice's most famous landmarks, is also located here. Santa Croce is a quieter area, offering a more relaxed pace of life and fewer tourists.

As you explore Venice, you'll notice that the city is a labyrinth of narrow streets, alleys, and canals. It's easy to get lost, but that's part of the charm. The best way to navigate Venice is on foot, as this allows you to discover hidden corners and charming squares that you might miss otherwise. Venice is a compact city, and you can walk from one end to the other in about an hour, but it's best to take your time and enjoy the journey.

Another way to get around is by using the vaporettos, Venice's water buses. These boats travel along the Grand Canal and connect the main islands of the city. The vaporettos are an essential part of life in Venice, and they offer a unique perspective of the city from the water. If you plan to use them frequently, consider buying a multi-day pass, which can save you money.

When navigating Venice, keep in mind that the city doesn't have a traditional street grid like most other places. Instead, streets are often named after the buildings or landmarks they lead to. For example, you might see signs for "Calle del Teatro" (Street of the Theater) or "Calle della Chiesa" (Street of the Church). This can make it tricky to find your way, but there are plenty of signs pointing to major landmarks like Rialto and San Marco. Following these signs can help you stay oriented.

Venice is also known for its bridges, the most famous being the Rialto Bridge and the Bridge of Sighs. Crossing these bridges is part of the Venetian experience, and they often lead to interesting neighborhoods and sights. The bridges are all different, with some offering stunning views of the canals, while others are small and simple, connecting quieter parts of the city.

If you get lost, don't worry—Venice is a safe city, and getting lost often leads to unexpected discoveries. You might stumble upon a quiet canal lined with flowers, a small café where locals gather, or a hidden courtyard filled with history. Embrace the adventure of exploring Venice's winding streets, and you'll find that every turn offers something new and beautiful.

Understanding the layout of Venice is key to making the most of your visit. The six districts each have their own unique appeal, and exploring them on foot or by vaporetto will give you a deeper appreciation of this extraordinary city. Don't be afraid to get lost; it's all part of the magic of Venice. With a bit of time and a sense of adventure, you'll soon feel at home navigating the enchanting maze of canals and streets that make Venice so special.

Duration of your trip

Deciding on the duration of your trip to Venice is an important step in planning your visit. The city is rich in history, art, and culture, and it offers a variety of experiences that can fit into different timeframes. Whether you have just a day or an entire week, Venice has something to offer every traveler.

If you only have one day in Venice, you'll need to focus on the highlights. Start early in the morning to make the most of your time. Begin your day at St. Mark's Square, where you can visit the iconic St. Mark's Basilica and the Doge's Palace. These landmarks are must-sees, offering a glimpse into Venice's glorious past. Afterward, take a walk along the Grand Canal and cross the Rialto Bridge. This is one of the most famous bridges in the world, and it offers stunning views of the canal. In the afternoon, consider taking a gondola ride or a vaporetto to see Venice from the water. Even with just one day, you'll get a taste of Venice's charm and beauty.

If you have two to three days in Venice, you can explore the city at a more relaxed pace. In addition to the main attractions, you'll have time to visit some of the lesser-known gems. Spend a morning in the Dorsoduro district, where you can visit the Peggy Guggenheim Collection, a museum of modern art housed in a beautiful palazzo. Nearby, you'll find the Accademia Gallery, which features an impressive collection of Venetian paintings. Take a stroll through the quiet streets of Cannaregio, where you can discover the Jewish Ghetto and enjoy a more local atmosphere. With a bit more time, you can also take a boat trip to the islands of Murano and Burano, famous for glassmaking and colorful houses, respectively. These islands offer a different perspective on Venice and are well worth a visit.

For those with four to five days, Venice truly opens up. You can dive deeper into the city's rich history and vibrant culture. Take the time to explore the Castello district, where you can visit the Arsenale, the historic shipyard that was once the heart of Venice's naval power. Wander through the Biennale Gardens, especially if your visit coincides with the Venice Biennale, an international art exhibition that attracts artists and visitors from around the world. You can also spend an afternoon at the Lido, Venice's beachside area, where you can relax by the sea and enjoy a different side of the city. With more days, you can take leisurely walks through Venice's many squares, enjoy long meals at local trattorias, and even revisit some of your favorite spots.

If you're fortunate enough to have a week or more in Venice, you can experience the city like a true Venetian. This amount of time allows you to explore each of the six districts (sestieri) in depth, discovering hidden corners and local secrets. You can take day trips to the nearby islands of Torcello, known for its ancient cathedral, and San Giorgio Maggiore, where you can climb the bell tower for panoramic views of the city. With a week, you can also delve into Venice's rich culinary scene, trying different restaurants, and perhaps even taking a cooking class to learn how to make traditional Venetian dishes. Consider attending a local event or festival, such as Carnevale, if your visit aligns with one. With a full week, you can truly immerse yourself in Venice's unique rhythm, enjoying its beauty and culture without feeling rushed.

No matter the length of your stay, it's important to allow some time for simply wandering. Venice is a city best explored on foot, and some of the most memorable experiences come from getting lost in its maze of streets and canals. Whether it's a day or a week, your time in Venice will be filled with moments of discovery and wonder.

The duration of your trip to Venice depends on your interests and schedule. A brief visit will give you a taste of the city's highlights, while a longer stay will allow you to explore in greater depth. Whatever you decide, Venice is a place that stays with you long after you've left, its beauty and charm lingering in your memory.

Venice on a budget

Exploring Venice on a budget is not only possible, but it can also be an incredibly rewarding experience. The city's rich history, stunning architecture, and vibrant culture are accessible to all travelers, even those looking to save money. With some thoughtful planning and a few insider tips, you can enjoy everything Venice has to offer without breaking the bank.

Timing your visit to Venice is one of the most important factors in keeping your trip affordable. The best times to visit for budget travelers are during the shoulder seasons—spring (April to June) and fall (September to November). During these periods, the weather is still pleasant, but the tourist crowds are thinner, leading to lower prices on accommodations and flights. You'll also find shorter lines at popular attractions, making it easier to explore without the stress of large crowds. Winter, especially from late November to early February, can also be an affordable time to visit Venice. While it can be chilly, the city is quiet, and you might even catch the magical sight of Venice covered in mist or lightly dusted with snow. However, avoid visiting during Carnevale, as prices soar and the city fills up with visitors from around the world.

When it comes to accommodation, Venice offers a range of budget-friendly options that don't sacrifice comfort. Staying in hostels is one of the most economical choices, with prices for a bed in a dormitory starting around €20-30 per night. Popular options include Generator Venice, located on the island of Giudecca, which offers stunning views of the Grand Canal, and

We_Crociferi, a stylish hostel housed in a renovated convent in the Cannaregio district. For a more private experience, consider guesthouses or budget hotels, where you can find double rooms starting around €60-80 per night. Another affordable option is vacation rentals, which can be particularly cost-effective if you're traveling with a group. Websites like Airbnb or Booking.com often have listings for entire apartments or shared spaces at reasonable rates, especially if you book well in advance. Staying in the less touristy areas like Mestre or the Lido can also help you save money, and the short commute into the city center is well worth the savings.

Activity planning in Venice doesn't have to be expensive. Many of the city's most famous attractions can be enjoyed for free or at a low cost. Start by exploring the city's iconic squares and bridges, such as St. Mark's Square and the Rialto Bridge. These landmarks are free to visit and offer endless opportunities for photography and people-watching. Walking around Venice is a joy in itself; the city's labyrinthine streets and canals are full of hidden gems waiting to be discovered. For art lovers, some of Venice's churches, like the Basilica di Santa Maria della Salute and the Church of San Giorgio Maggiore, house incredible works of art and can be visited for a small donation or entry fee. Additionally, consider purchasing a Museum Pass if you plan to visit multiple museums and galleries, as it offers significant savings. The pass typically costs around €25-30 and includes entry to a wide range of sites, including the Doge's Palace, the Correr Museum, and the Glass Museum in Murano.

Dining on a budget in Venice is easier than you might think, especially if you know where to look. Avoid eating in the tourist-heavy areas near St. Mark's Square, where prices are significantly inflated. Instead, venture into the neighborhoods where locals dine. Trattorias, osterias, and bacari (Venetian wine bars) offer traditional dishes at more reasonable prices. For a quick and affordable meal, try cicchetti, which are small tapas-like dishes typically served in bacari. You can enjoy a variety of these savory snacks for just a few euros each, paired with an ombra, a small glass of local wine. Another budget-friendly option is to buy fresh ingredients from the Rialto Market and have a picnic by one of the canals or in a quiet square. You can pick up bread, cheese, cold cuts, and fresh produce for a fraction of the cost of a restaurant meal and enjoy a leisurely lunch with a view. Don't forget to try a slice of pizza al taglio, Venice's version of pizza by the slice, which is both delicious and easy on the wallet.

For getting around Venice, the best way to save money is by walking. The city is small and designed for pedestrians, so you can easily explore most of the main attractions on foot. When you do need to use public transportation, the vaporetto (water bus) is the most affordable option. A single ride costs around €7.50, but if you plan on using the vaporetto frequently, consider purchasing a travel pass. These passes offer unlimited rides for a set period, with options for 24, 48, or 72 hours, and can save you a lot if you're hopping between islands or traveling longer distances. For an extra dose of local culture, take a traghetto across the Grand Canal. These are gondola-like boats that ferry passengers across the canal for just €2—a fraction of the cost of a traditional gondola ride.

Another tip is to carry a reusable water bottle. Venice has plenty of public fountains with fresh, drinkable water, so you can save money and reduce waste by refilling your bottle throughout the day.

Exploring Venice on a budget is all about timing your visit, choosing the right accommodations, and being smart about where and how you spend your money. By traveling during the shoulder seasons, opting for budget-friendly lodging, and enjoying the city's free or low-cost attractions, you can experience the magic of Venice without overspending. Dining like a local and taking advantage of affordable transportation options will help stretch your budget further. Remember, Venice's charm lies in its atmosphere, its unique blend of history and beauty, and the simple pleasure of wandering its streets. With careful planning and a few insider tips, you can create lasting memories in Venice without the need for lavish spending.

Essential Travel Tips

When traveling to Venice, having a few essential tips in mind can make your experience smoother and more enjoyable. Venice is a city like no other, with its winding canals, historic architecture, and vibrant culture. Here are some practical tips to help you navigate the city and make the most of your visit.

First, getting around Venice can be a bit tricky due to its unique layout. The city is built on a series of islands, connected by a maze of canals and narrow streets. To get the most out of your visit, it's helpful to embrace walking as your primary mode of transportation. Venice is a pedestrian-friendly city, and exploring on foot will allow you to discover hidden gems that you might miss if you only rely on public transportation. Comfortable shoes are a must, as you'll be doing a lot of walking on cobblestone streets.

Public transportation in Venice mainly consists of vaporettos, which are water buses that travel along the canals. While these can be convenient, they can also be expensive. Consider purchasing a travel pass if you plan to use the vaporetto frequently. This pass provides unlimited rides for a set number of days, which can be more cost-effective than buying single tickets each time you travel. For a more authentic experience, you might also try taking a traghetto, a gondola-like boat that crosses the Grand Canal for just a couple of euros.

Venice's labyrinthine layout means it's easy to get lost, but don't worry—that's part of the charm. Carry a good map or use a navigation app on your phone to help you find your way.

However, sometimes getting lost can lead you to unexpected discoveries, so don't be afraid to wander off the beaten path.

When it comes to dining, be aware that restaurants near major tourist attractions, such as St. Mark's Square, tend to be more expensive. For a more authentic and budget-friendly experience, seek out local eateries in less touristy neighborhoods. Trattorias and osterias often serve delicious Venetian cuisine at reasonable prices. You might also want to try cicchetti, Venetian tapas that you can enjoy with a glass of wine at a local bacaro.

If you plan to visit multiple museums or attractions, consider buying a Venice Pass. This pass typically offers discounted entry to several popular sites and can help you save money. Some attractions also offer free admission on certain days or times, so it's worth checking in advance to see if you can time your visit to take advantage of these opportunities.

Venice can be quite crowded, especially during peak tourist season. To avoid long lines and crowded areas, try to visit popular sites early in the morning or later in the afternoon. Additionally, weekdays are often less crowded than weekends.

Another tip is to stay hydrated and protect yourself from the sun. While Venice has many charming outdoor cafés where you can take a break and enjoy a drink, it's a good idea to carry a reusable water bottle with you, as the city has many public drinking fountains. If you're visiting during the summer, be sure to wear sunscreen and a hat, as it can get quite hot.

Be mindful of Venice's environmental efforts. The city is working hard to preserve its unique beauty and to manage the impact of tourism. Follow local guidelines, respect historical sites, and be conscious of your environmental footprint. For example, avoid taking unnecessary boat rides that contribute to water pollution and use refillable water bottles instead of buying plastic ones.

By keeping these tips in mind, you'll be well-prepared to enjoy all that Venice has to offer. The city's enchanting canals, historic buildings, and rich culture are best experienced with a relaxed and open mindset. Embrace the adventure of exploring Venice, and you're sure to have a memorable and enjoyable visit.

What to Pack for Venice

When preparing for a trip to Venice, packing wisely will help ensure you have a comfortable and enjoyable experience. The city's unique environment and varied weather mean that a little planning can go a long way. Here's a guide on what to pack for Venice, keeping in mind the city's distinctive characteristics and your comfort.

Start with clothing that suits the season you're visiting. Venice experiences four distinct seasons, each offering its own weather conditions. If you're visiting in the spring or fall, pack layers. Light sweaters, long-sleeve shirts, and a light jacket will help you stay comfortable as temperatures fluctuate throughout the day. For summer, choose lightweight, breathable clothing. Temperatures can soar, so pack comfortable shorts, t-shirts, and a wide-brimmed hat for sun protection. If you're traveling in winter, bring warm clothing, including a cozy coat, scarves, gloves, and hats. Venice can be chilly and damp during this time, so be prepared for colder temperatures and occasional rain.

Comfortable shoes are essential for Venice. The city's streets are often cobblestoned and uneven, making sturdy walking shoes a must. Opt for shoes that provide good support and are easy to walk in, as you'll likely be doing a lot of exploring on foot. Waterproof shoes or boots can also be helpful if you're visiting during the rainy season or in winter when the city can experience high tides that lead to flooding.

Don't forget a good umbrella. Venice is known for its occasional rain showers, and having an umbrella on hand can make a big difference. If you're visiting during the high-water season, sometimes called "acqua alta," waterproof boots or shoe covers can be useful to keep your feet dry.

Pack a reusable water bottle to stay hydrated while you explore. Venice has several public drinking fountains where you can refill your bottle throughout the day, which is both economical and environmentally friendly. Also, consider bringing a small, portable umbrella or rain jacket for unexpected rain showers.

If you plan to visit any religious sites or formal venues, pack modest clothing. Many churches and basilicas have dress codes that require shoulders and knees to be covered. A light scarf or shawl can be a handy addition for covering up when needed.

Traveling light is also advisable. Venice's narrow streets and numerous bridges mean that rolling luggage or large bags can be cumbersome. Consider using a small backpack or a crossbody bag for daily essentials. Keep important items such as your passport, money, and tickets secure and easily accessible.

Remember to pack your camera or smartphone for capturing the stunning views and memorable moments. Venice is incredibly picturesque, with its canals, historic buildings, and unique ambiance, so you'll want to have a way to document your adventures.

By packing thoughtfully and considering the unique aspects of Venice, you'll be well-prepared to enjoy all the city has to offer. Comfortable clothing, sturdy shoes, and practical items will ensure that you're ready for everything Venice has in store.

Choosing the right tour package

Selecting the best tour package for Venice can greatly enhance your travel experience, ensuring that you get the most out of your visit to this enchanting city. With so many options available, it's important to understand the different types of tour packages and what each offers. Here's a comprehensive guide to help you choose the right tour package for your trip to Venice.

There are several types of tour packages you can consider. Guided tours are one of the most popular options. These typically include a knowledgeable guide who will lead you through key sites and provide insights into Venice's history, culture, and architecture. Guided tours can be comprehensive, covering major attractions like St. Mark's Basilica and the Doge's Palace, or they can focus on specific interests such as art, history, or cuisine. These tours usually last between 2 to 4 hours and can range in cost from around 50 to 150 euros per person, depending on the inclusions and length.

Self-guided walking tours are another option. These tours provide you with a map and itinerary, allowing you to explore Venice at your own pace. This type of tour is ideal for those who prefer a flexible schedule and enjoy the freedom to stop and explore on their own. Self-guided tours are generally less expensive, with costs ranging from 20 to 50 euros, and can include audio guides or app-based navigation to enhance the experience.

Adventure excursions cater to travelers seeking unique and active experiences. These might include gondola rides, cycling tours, or even kayaking through Venice's canals. These packages often combine sightseeing with an element of adventure and can vary widely in duration and cost. A gondola ride might be part of a larger tour costing around 100 euros, while a more extensive excursion involving multiple activities could be priced at 200 euros or more.

When selecting a tour package, consider the duration, cost, and what is included. Guided tours typically last a few hours and may include entrance fees to attractions, transportation, and sometimes even meals. Self-guided tours usually provide a map and suggested route, and may include discounts or vouchers for local attractions. Adventure excursions vary in length, often spanning a few hours to a full day, and usually include equipment and guides.

Traveler suitability plays a significant role in choosing the right package. Families might appreciate guided tours that are designed to be engaging for all ages, including child-friendly activities and explanations. Couples often enjoy romantic gondola rides or intimate walking tours that allow for a leisurely exploration of Venice's charming streets. Solo travelers might prefer self-guided tours for the flexibility and independence they offer, while groups might benefit from private guided tours that can accommodate larger numbers and provide a more personalized experience.

Seasonal considerations are important when planning your tour. Venice experiences different crowd levels and weather conditions throughout the year. In the peak summer months, tours can be crowded and more expensive, but they also offer the advantage of long daylight hours and a lively atmosphere. In contrast, the off-season, such as winter, can provide a more relaxed experience with fewer tourists and potentially lower prices. However, some tours might be limited or unavailable during the off-season, so it's essential to check availability and plan accordingly.

Local insights can offer valuable perspectives when choosing a tour package. Local guides often share unique stories and hidden gems that aren't always covered in standard tours. Previous travelers might recommend lesser-known tours that provide a more authentic experience away from the typical tourist spots. Exploring reviews and seeking recommendations from locals can help you discover these unique opportunities.

When booking a tour package, look for reputable tour operators and read reviews to ensure a quality experience. Many tour operators offer online booking options, allowing you to compare prices and packages easily. It's also beneficial to book in advance, especially during peak travel seasons, to secure your preferred tour and avoid last-minute availability issues.

Personalization and flexibility can greatly enhance your travel experience. Some tour packages offer customization options, allowing you to tailor the itinerary to your preferences. Combining different tours can also create a more comprehensive experience, such as pairing a guided walking tour with a gondola ride or adding a food tasting tour to your itinerary.

Choosing the right tour package for Venice involves considering your interests, budget, and travel style. By researching and understanding the various options available, you can select a tour that aligns with your preferences and ensures a memorable visit to this magical city. With careful planning and a bit of flexibility, you'll be able to enjoy all the unique and enchanting experiences Venice has to offer.

Entry and visa requirements

Navigating entry and visa requirements can seem daunting, but understanding the process can make your travel experience smoother and more enjoyable. Here's a comprehensive guide to help you through visa requirements and the application process.

Determining whether you need a visa for your destination involves checking the entry requirements for the country or countries you plan to visit. Most countries require a visa if you are staying for a period longer than a specified duration or if you are traveling for specific purposes like work or study. For European destinations, the Schengen visa is a common requirement for many travelers. This visa allows for short stays of up to 90 days within a 180-day period in the Schengen Area, which includes 26 European countries. To find out if you need a visa, consult the embassy or consulate of the country you are visiting or use official visa information websites.

Once you determine that you need a visa, the application process begins. Here is a step-by-step guide to help you through:

1. Check Visa Requirements: Visit the official website of the embassy or consulate of the country you are visiting. This site will provide specific details on visa types and requirements.

Make sure to use official government websites to avoid misinformation.

2. Gather Required Documents: Typically, you will need your passport, recent passport-sized photographs, travel itinerary, proof of accommodation, and evidence of financial means. Each country may have additional requirements, so check the specific guidelines for the visa you are applying for.

3. Complete the Application Form: Fill out the visa application form, which can usually be downloaded from the embassy's website or obtained directly from their office. Ensure that all information is accurate and matches your supporting documents.

4. Submit Your Application: Depending on the country, you may need to submit your application in person at an embassy or consulate, or you might be able to apply online. Follow the specific instructions provided by the embassy or consulate.

5. Pay the Visa Fee: There will typically be a fee associated with the visa application. This fee can vary depending on the type of visa and the country you are applying to. Check the exact amount and acceptable payment methods on the embassy's website.

6. Attend an Interview (if required): Some visa applications may require an interview at the embassy or consulate. Be prepared to answer questions about your travel plans and provide additional documentation if requested.

7. Wait for Processing: Visa processing times can vary. The embassy or consulate will provide an estimated processing time, which can range from a few days to several weeks. Plan your application well in advance of your travel date.

8. Receive Your Visa: Once your visa is approved, you will receive a visa sticker or stamp in your passport. Check the details to ensure that all information is correct and that the visa covers your travel dates.

For a smooth visa application process, consider these practical tips:

- Start Early: Begin your visa application process well in advance of your planned travel date. This allows ample time for gathering documents, processing, and any potential delays.

- Use Official Resources: Always rely on official government websites for the most accurate and up-to-date visa information.

- Double-Check Documentation: Ensure that all required documents are complete and accurate before submission. Missing or incorrect documents can delay the processing of your visa.

To make the process clearer, imagine a traveler from the United States planning a trip to Italy. The U.S. citizen would need to apply for a Schengen visa, as Italy is part of the Schengen Area. They would gather their passport, complete the application form, provide proof of travel insurance, show their travel itinerary, and submit the application at the nearest Italian consulate. The process might differ slightly for a traveler from Australia or Brazil, with variations in required documents or processing times, but the overall steps remain similar.

Understanding and following the visa requirements and application process carefully can ensure a hassle-free travel experience. By planning ahead and using official resources, you can navigate entry and visa requirements effectively and focus on enjoying your journey.

CHAPTER 2.
GETTING TO VENICE

Choosing the Best flights

Selecting the best flights to Venice requires a blend of research, flexibility, and strategic planning. Here's a comprehensive guide to help you navigate your options and find the perfect flight for your trip.

Venice's primary airport is Marco Polo Airport (VCE), which serves as the main gateway for international travelers. Several major airlines offer direct flights to Venice, including Emirates, Lufthansa, British Airways, and Alitalia. These airlines typically provide service from major hubs such as New York, London, Frankfurt, and Dubai. Flights from North America usually take around 8 to 10 hours, while flights from other European cities might be shorter, ranging from 1.5 to 3 hours. Each airline has its own service standards, with variations in comfort, onboard amenities, and ticket pricing, so it's worthwhile to compare them before booking.

To find the best deals on flights, it's important to start by booking well in advance. Airfares often increase as the departure date approaches, so securing your tickets several months ahead can save you money. Flexibility with travel dates can also be advantageous. Prices can fluctuate based on demand, so traveling mid-week or during off-peak seasons often results in lower fares. Using price comparison websites like Skyscanner or Google Flights allows you to easily compare prices across different airlines and find the best deals. Setting fare alerts can notify you when prices drop, and taking advantage of airline sales and promotions can provide additional savings.

Flight prices and availability can vary significantly with the seasons. The peak tourist season in Venice is during the summer months, particularly June through August, when flights are often more expensive and harder to come by. For the best value, consider traveling during the shoulder seasons, such as spring (April to June) or fall (September to October). These times generally offer pleasant weather and lower prices. Winter, while less crowded, can also be a good time to visit if you don't mind cooler temperatures.

When flying to Venice, travelers should be aware of potential airport fees and taxes. These can include security fees, airport improvement charges, and other surcharges that might be added to the ticket price. To minimize these costs, look for flights that include all fees in the price rather than adding them separately at checkout. Be sure to check the airline's policies to avoid surprises.

Baggage policies can vary widely among airlines. Most major airlines include a carry-on bag and a personal item in the ticket price, but checked baggage usually comes with an additional fee. The weight limits and fees for checked baggage vary, so it's important to review the airline's policy before packing. If you have oversized or additional luggage, consider paying for extra baggage in advance, which is often cheaper than paying at the airport.

Different travel classes offer varying levels of comfort and amenities. Economy class is the most basic and affordable option, while premium economy provides extra legroom and added comfort for a higher price. Business class offers a more luxurious experience with better seating, premium food, and priority boarding. First class is the most exclusive, with top-tier services and amenities. Depending on your budget and preferences, choosing the right class can enhance your travel experience.

When booking your flight, consider the best time to purchase. Generally, booking mid-week and avoiding major holiday periods can yield better prices. Navigate airline websites carefully, ensuring you understand the terms and conditions of your ticket, including cancellation policies and potential fees. Investing in travel insurance can provide peace of mind in case of unexpected changes or cancellations.

Frequent travelers might benefit from enrolling in airline loyalty programs. These programs offer rewards, such as points or miles, which can be redeemed for future flights, upgrades, or other perks. By accumulating points, you can enjoy benefits like priority boarding, access to airport lounges, and complimentary upgrades.

Selecting the best flights to Venice involves considering various factors such as airline options, seasonal variations, baggage policies, and travel classes. Thorough research and planning will help you find a flight that meets your needs and budget, ensuring a smooth and enjoyable start to your Venetian adventure. By following these tips, you can make informed decisions and maximize your travel experience.

Venice airport: Arrival and Orientation

Arriving in Venice begins with landing at Marco Polo Airport (VCE), the main airport serving this enchanting city. As your plane descends, you'll notice the unique landscape of Venice, with its intricate network of canals and historic buildings.

Upon arrival at Marco Polo Airport, you'll first need to go through passport control, especially if you're coming from outside the Schengen Area. After that, follow the signs to baggage claim if you have checked luggage. The airport is well-organized, and the signage is clear, so you should find your way easily. Once you have your bags, you'll proceed to the arrivals hall.

In the arrivals hall, you'll find various services and facilities to help you get started with your trip. If you need to exchange currency or withdraw cash, there are several ATMs and currency exchange counters available. There's also a tourist information desk where you can get maps, brochures, and advice on how to get to your destination in Venice.

To get to the city, you have several options. The most convenient and popular method is the water taxi. These taxis provide a direct and scenic route to Venice's historic center, offering a unique view of the city's canals as you travel. Tickets for water taxis can be purchased at the airport or in advance online. Another option is the Alilaguna water bus service, which is a more economical choice but might take longer since it makes several stops along the way.

If you prefer to travel by land, there are regular buses that connect the airport to Venice's mainland train station, Venezia Santa Lucia. From there, you can take a train or a Vaporetto (water bus) to reach various parts of Venice. You can also opt for a private transfer or taxi service, though taxis are less common in Venice due to the city's unique layout.

In the airport, you'll also find several dining options, shops, and facilities such as baggage storage if you need to leave your luggage while you explore the city. The airport is well-equipped to handle travelers' needs, and the staff is generally helpful if you have any questions.

As you start your journey into Venice, you'll quickly notice the charm and vibrancy of the city. The combination of historic architecture, winding canals, and lively atmosphere will make your arrival a memorable experience. Make sure to take a moment to enjoy the view and get excited about the adventures that await you in Venice.

Journey to Venice

Starting your journey to Venice is like preparing for a trip to a city unlike any other in the world. The excitement begins the moment you decide to visit this magical place, known for its romantic canals, stunning architecture, and rich history. Whether you're traveling by air, train, or car, the journey to Venice is an adventure in itself.

If you're flying to Venice, you'll most likely land at Marco Polo Airport. From here, the city is just a short distance away. As your plane descends, you might catch your first glimpse of Venice from above, with its maze of canals and historic buildings spread out below. Once you land, you'll find the airport well-organized, with clear signs to help you reach your next mode of transportation, whether it's a water taxi, a bus, or a train.

Traveling by train is another popular way to reach Venice, especially if you're coming from within Europe. The main train station, Venezia Santa Lucia, is located right on the edge of the Grand Canal. As your train pulls into the station, you'll step out into the heart of Venice, immediately surrounded by the city's unique atmosphere. The train ride itself can be quite scenic, especially if you're traveling from nearby cities like Milan or Florence, offering beautiful views of the Italian countryside.

For those who prefer driving, you can reach Venice by car, but it's important to know that the city is car-free.

You'll need to park your car in one of the parking facilities in Piazzale Roma, the last point where vehicles are allowed. From there, you'll continue your journey into Venice on foot or by water transport. Driving to Venice can be a great way to explore the surrounding areas before reaching the city, but once you arrive, be prepared to navigate the city on foot or by boat.

No matter how you arrive, the moment you set foot in Venice, you'll feel the city's unique charm. The lack of cars, the sound of water lapping against the buildings, and the sight of gondolas gliding through the canals all create a sense of stepping back in time. Your journey to Venice doesn't end when you arrive—it's just the beginning of an experience that will stay with you long after you leave.

As you explore Venice, you'll discover that getting around is part of the adventure. The city's narrow alleys, historic bridges, and winding canals create a labyrinth that invites you to wander and explore. Whether you're walking along the cobblestone streets or taking a Vaporetto (water bus) down the Grand Canal, each journey offers new sights and experiences.

In Venice, every step is a journey through history, art, and culture. From the bustling St. Mark's Square to the quieter, hidden corners of the city, there's always something new to discover. Embrace the adventure and let yourself get lost in the beauty of Venice—you never know what you might find just around the corner.

Train Options

Traveling to Venice by train is a delightful and convenient way to reach this iconic city. The train journey itself often becomes a memorable part of the trip, with scenic views and a relaxed pace that allows you to enjoy the Italian countryside.

Several train options are available depending on where you are starting your journey. If you're coming from within Italy or nearby European countries, you'll find that Venice is well-connected by a network of high-speed and regional trains. These trains are efficient, comfortable, and offer a stress-free way to travel.

For those traveling from other major Italian cities, like Rome, Milan, or Florence, high-speed trains operated by Trenitalia or Italo are the best choices. These trains, known as Frecciarossa, Frecciargento, and Frecciabianca, can reach speeds of up to 300 kilometers per hour, making the journey to Venice fast and smooth. The Frecciarossa trains, in particular, are known for their modern amenities, including spacious seating, Wi-Fi, and onboard dining options. These trains also offer different classes, from standard to first class, allowing you to choose the level of comfort that suits your needs.

If you're coming from a nearby country like Austria, Switzerland, or France, international trains such as the EuroCity or Thello offer direct services to Venice. These trains provide a scenic journey through the Alps and across beautiful landscapes, making the trip an enjoyable part of your adventure. The EuroCity trains are particularly popular for their comfort and the stunning views they offer, especially if you're traveling through the mountains.

For those already in Italy, regional trains are a more affordable option. While they may take a bit longer than the high-speed trains, they stop at smaller towns and villages along the way, giving you a chance to see more of Italy's charming countryside. These trains are perfect if you're in no hurry and want to explore different parts of the country before arriving in Venice.

Once you arrive at Venezia Santa Lucia, the main train station in Venice, you'll step out directly into the heart of the city. The station is located right on the Grand Canal, offering a stunning first glimpse of Venice. From here, you can easily access water taxis, Vaporetto (water buses), or simply start exploring on foot.

Booking your train tickets in advance is a good idea, especially if you're traveling during peak tourist seasons or on popular routes. This ensures you get the best prices and your preferred seat. Most train companies offer online booking, where you can compare schedules, prices, and choose your class of service.

Traveling to Venice by train combines comfort, convenience, and the chance to see more of Italy's beautiful scenery. Whether you're coming from another part of Italy or from across Europe, the train journey to Venice sets the stage for the enchanting experience that awaits you in this remarkable city.

Bus Options

Traveling to Venice by bus is a practical and often economical option, especially if you're coming from nearby cities or other European countries. The bus journey allows you to see more of the countryside and can be a comfortable way to reach this iconic destination.

Several bus companies operate routes to Venice, connecting it with other major Italian cities and European capitals. If you're traveling from cities like Milan, Florence, or Bologna, you'll find frequent bus services that offer a straightforward and budget-friendly way to reach Venice. These buses usually have modern amenities such as air conditioning, Wi-Fi, and comfortable seating, making the journey pleasant and relaxing.

For those coming from other parts of Europe, international bus companies like FlixBus and Eurolines offer services to Venice. These buses often run overnight, allowing you to sleep during the journey and arrive in Venice refreshed and ready to explore. The routes from cities like Munich, Vienna, or Ljubljana are particularly popular, providing a convenient link to Venice without the hassle of multiple transfers.

When you arrive by bus, your likely destination will be Piazzale Roma, the main bus terminal in Venice. This bustling square is the gateway to the city, and from here, you can easily connect to the rest of Venice. Piazzale Roma is located right next to the Grand Canal, making it easy to hop on a Vaporetto (water bus) or take a short walk to many of the city's attractions.

One of the advantages of traveling by bus is the flexibility in routes and schedules. Buses often offer more frequent departures and can be a good choice if you're booking last minute or if train options are limited. Additionally, buses tend to be more affordable than trains, especially for those on a tight budget. Many bus companies offer promotional fares and discounts, particularly if you book in advance or travel during off-peak times.

It's important to check the baggage policy when traveling by bus, as different companies may have varying rules. Most long-distance buses allow you to bring one or two pieces of luggage, but it's always a good idea to confirm the details before you travel to avoid any surprises.

Booking your bus ticket online is straightforward and allows you to compare prices, schedules, and services. Some companies even offer mobile tickets, so you don't need to print anything out. Just show your ticket on your phone when boarding.

While buses may take longer than trains, they provide a more scenic and leisurely journey, often stopping in smaller towns along the way. This can be a great opportunity to see parts of Italy or Europe that you might otherwise miss.

Taking the bus to Venice is a practical, cost-effective, and sometimes scenic way to travel. Whether you're coming from within Italy or from another European country, the bus journey adds to the overall experience, bringing you to the magical city of Venice in comfort and style.

Any other travel option for Venice

If you're planning a trip to Venice, there are several other travel options beyond trains and buses that can make your journey both convenient and enjoyable. Each option has its own set of advantages, depending on your starting point, budget, and personal preferences.

One of the most popular ways to reach Venice is by car. Driving allows you to travel at your own pace, making stops along the way to explore charming Italian towns and picturesque landscapes. However, it's important to note that Venice itself is a car-free city. If you choose to drive, you'll need to park your car in one of the parking facilities located at the edge of the city, such as Tronchetto or Piazzale Roma. From there, you can take a Vaporetto (water bus) or walk to your accommodation. Driving can be a good option if you're traveling with a lot of luggage or if you want the flexibility to explore other parts of Italy before or after your visit to Venice.

For those coming from international destinations, flying is often the quickest and most direct way to reach Venice. Venice Marco Polo Airport is the main airport serving the city, with flights from major European cities and beyond. Once you arrive at the airport, you can take a water taxi, Vaporetto, or bus to reach the heart of Venice. There is also the option of landing at Treviso Airport, which is smaller and primarily serves budget airlines. From Treviso, you can easily reach Venice by bus or shuttle service.

Another option for arriving in Venice is by boat, especially if you're traveling from other parts of Italy or the Mediterranean. Venice is a major port for cruise ships, and many travelers arrive in the city as part of a Mediterranean cruise itinerary. If you're traveling by ferry from destinations like Greece, Croatia, or the Adriatic coast, you'll find several services that dock in Venice. Arriving by boat offers a unique perspective of the city as you sail into the lagoon, with the stunning architecture and iconic canals greeting you as you approach.

Bicycling is another option for the more adventurous traveler, particularly if you're already in Italy or one of the neighboring countries. While Venice itself is not suited for cycling due to its narrow streets and numerous bridges, you can ride your bike to the edge of the city and park it in designated areas before exploring Venice on foot. Cycling can be an enjoyable and environmentally friendly way to travel, especially if you're looking to take in the scenic routes along the way.

If you're looking for a more luxurious and leisurely way to travel, consider taking a private car service or a chauffeured vehicle. This option offers the convenience of door-to-door service, allowing you to relax and enjoy the journey without worrying about navigating or parking. Private car services can be arranged from major cities in Italy, and while they are more expensive than public transportation options, they provide comfort and a personalized experience.

Finally, for those who prefer a slower pace, walking can be a viable option if you're staying relatively close to Venice or within the Veneto region. While it may not be the quickest way to reach the city, walking allows you to fully immerse yourself in the Italian countryside and discover hidden gems along the way. You can combine walking with other forms of transportation, such as taking a train or bus for part of the journey and then walking the final stretch into Venice.

Each of these travel options offers its own unique experience, and choosing the right one depends on your personal preferences and travel plans. Whether you prefer the speed of a plane, the flexibility of a car, or the scenic journey of a boat, there's a travel option that will make your trip to Venice unforgettable.

CHAPTER 2.
GETTING AROUND VENICE

Vaporetto: The Public Water Bus System

The Vaporetto in Venice's public water bus system and a unique way to get around this enchanting city. It's an essential part of Venetian life and a convenient method for tourists to explore various parts of Venice and its surrounding islands.

The Vaporetto operates much like a traditional bus system, but instead of driving on roads, these boats glide along the city's canals and waterways. They are a popular choice for both locals and visitors because they offer a picturesque and practical way to travel. The Vaporetto connects major points of interest across Venice, including popular spots like St. Mark's Square, the Rialto Bridge, and the islands of Murano, Burano, and Torcello.

The boats are designed to accommodate a decent number of passengers, and you'll find them running frequently throughout the day. There are different lines or routes, each serving specific areas or destinations. For example, Line 1 and Line 2 are commonly used by tourists as they travel along the Grand Canal, offering stunning views of the historic buildings lining the canal.

When you plan to use the Vaporetto, it's important to know how to buy tickets and understand the pricing. Tickets can be purchased at Vaporetto ticket booths, which are located at major stops and stations, or through automated machines. You can also buy tickets online in advance. Prices vary depending on the type of ticket you choose, whether it's for a single journey or a pass for multiple days. There are options for one-way tickets, multi-day passes, and even special tickets for tourists that include discounts on various attractions.

To make your trip comfortable and smooth, here are a few practical tips. First, keep an eye on the Vaporetto schedule, as the frequency of boats can vary depending on the time of day and the specific line you're using. During peak tourist seasons, the boats can get quite crowded, so be prepared for a bit of a squeeze, especially during rush hours.

It's also a good idea to plan your route ahead of time. The Vaporetto map can be a helpful tool to understand which lines to take to reach your desired destinations. For tourists, it's worth noting that some lines, like the one that travels along the Grand Canal, offer a scenic journey that's almost as enjoyable as the destinations themselves.

In terms of practicalities, make sure to validate your ticket before boarding. This is usually done by stamping your ticket at designated machines at the dock. Once on board, you'll find seating both inside and outside the boat. If you can, grab a seat outside for the best views of Venice's beautiful architecture and bustling canal life.

Using the Vaporetto is not just a means of transportation but an experience in itself. It allows you to see Venice from a unique perspective and provides a glimpse into the daily rhythm of life in this water-bound city. By taking the Vaporetto, you'll effortlessly navigate the canals, enjoy some breathtaking views, and immerse yourself in the distinctive charm of Venice's waterways.

Gondolas: A Traditional Ride

Gondolas are one of Venice's most iconic symbols, offering a quintessentially Venetian experience. These sleek, black boats are traditionally used for navigating the narrow canals of the city, and taking a gondola ride is a memorable way to experience Venice's charm and beauty.

The gondola itself is a work of art. It's a long, narrow boat with a distinctive shape, designed to glide smoothly through the canals. Each gondola is hand-crafted and traditionally painted black, although the details can vary. The gondola is steered by a gondolier who stands at the stern and uses a single, long oar to propel the boat forward. Gondoliers are often dressed in classic striped shirts and straw hats, adding to the picturesque charm of the ride.

When you embark on a gondola ride, you're in for a serene and romantic journey through Venice's labyrinth of canals. The ride takes you through quiet, picturesque waterways and beneath charming bridges, allowing you to see parts of Venice that are often inaccessible by other means. The gondola's gentle sway and the gondolier's rhythmic rowing create a soothing and leisurely experience.

Gondola rides are typically available throughout the day, but many people prefer to take a ride in the late afternoon or early evening when the light softens and the canals are less crowded. This can add to the magical atmosphere of the ride. Some gondoliers also offer evening rides, which can be particularly enchanting with the city lights reflecting on the water.

The cost of a gondola ride can vary depending on the length of the ride and the time of day. A standard gondola ride usually lasts about 30 to 40 minutes and costs a set amount per gondola, not per person. Prices can be higher during peak tourist season or during evening hours. It's also common for gondoliers to offer longer rides or special packages, so it's worth asking if you're interested in an extended experience or a private tour of specific canals.

When planning a gondola ride, it's a good idea to book in advance if you're visiting during peak times or if you have specific preferences. However, you can also find gondola rides available on a walk-up basis, especially near popular spots like St. Mark's Square or the Rialto Bridge.

For a truly authentic experience, consider discussing your preferences with your gondolier. Some gondoliers may share interesting stories or facts about the canals and the city, making your ride even more enjoyable. And, of course, don't forget to bring a camera to capture the stunning views and the timeless beauty of Venice.

Taking a gondola ride in Venice is more than just a tour; it's a romantic and nostalgic journey that lets you soak in the city's unique atmosphere. It's a chance to relax and enjoy the tranquil beauty of Venice's canals while being gently glided along by a skilled gondolier. Whether you're on a romantic getaway, a family adventure, or simply exploring the wonders of Venice, a gondola ride is an experience you'll treasure.

Walking in Venice: Tips for Exploring on Foot

Walking in Venice is like stepping into a living postcard. The city's enchanting canals, charming alleys, and historic buildings are best experienced on foot. Exploring Venice by walking allows you to discover hidden gems and appreciate the city's unique atmosphere at a leisurely pace.

As you set out on your walk, you'll notice that Venice is a maze of narrow streets and quaint squares. While this might seem confusing at first, it's part of the city's charm. The winding pathways lead to delightful surprises, like picturesque canals and small shops selling Venetian crafts. It's worth having a good map or a navigation app, but don't be afraid to get a little lost. Sometimes the best discoveries are made off the beaten path.

Comfortable shoes are essential for walking in Venice. The city is made up of cobblestone streets and bridges, which can be tough on your feet if you're wearing anything but sturdy walking shoes. Opt for shoes that are supportive and can handle a bit of uneven terrain. Additionally, be prepared for lots of walking—Venice is best explored at a leisurely pace, so make sure you're ready for a day of strolling.

Venice's canals and bridges add a unique twist to walking around. You'll frequently cross over charming bridges that span the canals. Some of these bridges have steps, so be cautious if you're carrying a lot of luggage or if you have mobility issues. It's helpful to pack lightly and bring a small backpack or tote for essentials.

One of the joys of walking in Venice is the opportunity to enjoy spontaneous moments. Take time to stop at a café for a coffee or gelato, or pause to admire the views along the canals. Many of Venice's most iconic landmarks, like St. Mark's Basilica and the Rialto Bridge, are best appreciated from the street level. Walking gives you the chance to really take in the architectural details and vibrant street life.

Also, consider visiting Venice's different neighborhoods. Each area has its own character and attractions. For example, the San Marco area is famous for its grand architecture and bustling squares, while neighborhoods like Cannaregio and Dorsoduro offer a more laid-back, local feel. Walking between these areas lets you see a variety of Venice's personalities.

It's important to stay hydrated, especially if you're visiting during the warmer months. There are plenty of places to grab a drink or a bite to eat along your route. Keep a bottle of water with you and take breaks when needed. Venice can get quite warm, so wearing light, breathable clothing will also keep you comfortable.

Finally, be aware of your surroundings. Venice is a safe city, but like in any popular tourist destination, it's wise to keep an eye on your belongings and be mindful of pickpockets. Always be respectful of the local customs and enjoy the leisurely pace of life in this beautiful city.

Walking in Venice is a delightful way to immerse yourself in the city's rich history and vibrant culture. Each step takes you deeper into a world of timeless beauty, where every corner holds a story and every canal offers a new perspective. So lace up those comfortable shoes, grab a map, and set out to explore Venice on foot—you're in for an unforgettable experience.

Venice by Bicycle: Exploring the Lido

Exploring Venice by bicycle offers a refreshing change of pace from the traditional walking tours, especially when you venture out to the Lido, a long, narrow island just a short ferry ride from the main city. The Lido provides a unique opportunity to experience a different side of Venice, with its beautiful beaches, wide open spaces, and charming local neighborhoods.

The Lido is known for its relaxed atmosphere compared to the bustling center of Venice. It's a great place to enjoy a leisurely bike ride. You can rent a bicycle from various shops on the Lido itself or in Venice before taking the Vaporetto (water bus) over to the island. Many rental shops offer reasonable rates, and some even provide bike helmets and maps to help you navigate the island.

Cycling on the Lido is quite pleasant due to its flat terrain and well-maintained paths. As you ride along, you'll find yourself surrounded by lush greenery and the serene environment of the island. The Lido is famous for its long, sandy beaches. Riding along the waterfront, you'll have the chance to enjoy stunning views of the Adriatic Sea. There are several beach clubs where you can stop for a swim or simply relax by the sea. Some of the beaches require an entrance fee, but there are also free public beaches where you can enjoy the sun and sand.

The island is also home to lovely residential neighborhoods and quaint local shops. Cycling through these areas offers a glimpse into everyday Venetian life away from the tourist crowds. You might come across charming cafes where you can stop for a coffee or a light meal, as well as local markets where you can pick up fresh produce or souvenirs.

One of the highlights of biking on the Lido is exploring its unique natural landscapes. The island is dotted with parks and green spaces perfect for a leisurely ride. The Lagoon of Venice, visible from various points on the island, adds to the scenic beauty. You'll find that cycling allows you to cover more ground and see more of the island's diverse scenery in a shorter time.

When biking on the Lido, it's wise to plan your route ahead of time. While the island is not very large, having a general idea of where you want to go can help you make the most of your visit. There are several bike-friendly paths and designated lanes, but being aware of your surroundings and other cyclists will ensure a safe and enjoyable experience.

In terms of packing for your bike ride, make sure to bring sunscreen, a hat, and plenty of water, especially if you're visiting during the warmer months. Even though the Lido has many spots to stop and relax, staying hydrated and protected from the sun will keep your ride comfortable.

Overall, biking on the Lido offers a unique way to explore Venice that combines the charm of the island's natural beauty with the convenience of cycling. It's an enjoyable and active way to see a different side of Venice, making your visit all the more memorable. So grab a bike, hop on a Vaporetto, and discover the relaxed, picturesque world of the Lido at your own pace.

Water Taxis: Private and Group Services

Water taxis in Venice offer a convenient and charming way to navigate the city's intricate waterways. These boats provide both private and group services, each catering to different needs and preferences. Whether you're looking for a personalized experience or a shared journey, water taxis can enhance your visit to Venice.

Private water taxis are an excellent choice if you prefer a more exclusive and flexible mode of transportation. These taxis can be hired for individual trips or to transport groups of travelers. They offer a more private and comfortable way to travel, with the added benefit of being able to set your own schedule. You can arrange a private water taxi to pick you up from the airport or train station and deliver you directly to your hotel or any other destination within Venice. It's a stress-free way to start or end your trip, as you won't need to deal with the crowded public transport system or haul your luggage through busy streets.

To book a private water taxi, you can use online services or contact local companies directly. Many companies offer online booking options, where you can choose the type of boat and schedule your pickup. Pricing can vary depending on the distance, the size of the boat, and the time of day. It's a good idea to compare a few options and read reviews to ensure you're getting a reliable service.

Group water taxis provide a cost-effective alternative for traveling with others. These services operate on a shared basis, meaning you'll be sharing the boat with other passengers who are traveling in the same direction. Group water taxis are typically used for common routes, such as transfers between the airport, train station, and central Venice. They're a great option if you're traveling with a small group and want to save on transportation costs while still enjoying the unique experience of traveling by water.

Group water taxis can also be hired for tours or private events. This option allows you to enjoy a scenic ride through Venice's canals and lagoon, with the added benefit of having a dedicated boat for your group. It's a wonderful way to celebrate special occasions or simply to explore the city from a different perspective.

When using water taxis, it's helpful to know a few things to make your journey smooth. Always check the departure and arrival points beforehand, as water taxi stops are located throughout the city. Be prepared for a potentially higher price compared to other modes of transport, especially for private services. However, the experience of gliding through Venice's canals and seeing the city from the water makes it well worth the cost.

Whether you choose a private water taxi for a personalized journey or a group service for a more economical option, both provide a distinctive and enjoyable way to explore Venice. The charm of traveling by water, combined with the convenience of tailored services, ensures that your trip through the city's canals is both memorable and hassle-free.

Navigating the Canals

Navigating the canals of Venice is one of the most enchanting experiences you can have while visiting the city. The canals serve as the main thoroughfares of Venice, and traveling along them offers a unique perspective of this beautiful, historic city.

The Grand Canal is the largest and most famous of Venice's waterways. It curves through the heart of the city, lined with grand palaces and bustling markets. A ride along the Grand Canal gives you a view of Venice's architectural splendor, with its magnificent buildings and vibrant life. You can hop on a Vaporetto, which is the public water bus service, for an affordable and scenic trip. The Vaporetto stops at various points along the Grand Canal, allowing you to hop on and off as you explore different areas.

For a more intimate experience, consider taking a private water taxi or gondola ride. These options provide a personalized journey through the quieter canals and hidden corners of Venice. Gondolas, in particular, offer a romantic and leisurely way to glide through narrow, winding canals that are less frequented by larger boats. The gentle sway of the gondola and the skillful maneuvering by the gondolier create a serene atmosphere, perfect for a relaxing exploration of the city's more secluded waterways.

As you navigate the canals, you'll come across several smaller and lesser-known canals. These smaller waterways are the lifelines of local Venice, revealing picturesque scenes of daily Venetian life. You might see locals transporting goods or catching glimpses of charming, hidden courtyards and quaint houses. It's an excellent way to get a feel for the true essence of Venice, away from the more tourist-heavy areas.

When traveling by boat, keep in mind that the canals are the primary routes for all kinds of water transport, so they can get quite busy, especially during peak tourist seasons. Be prepared for some congestion, particularly around popular spots like Piazza San Marco and the Rialto Bridge. However, this bustle also adds to the lively atmosphere of Venice, making it a vibrant experience.

For those who want to explore Venice more actively, renting a kayak or paddleboard is another exciting option. This gives you the freedom to navigate the canals at your own pace, offering a hands-on way to see the city. Paddling through the canals allows you to access even more secluded areas, providing a sense of adventure and discovery.

To make the most of your canal exploration, it's a good idea to familiarize yourself with Venice's layout and canal routes. Maps and guides are available that show the major canals and key landmarks, which can help you plan your journey. Also, consider the time of day you choose to navigate the canals; early morning or late afternoon often provides a quieter and more picturesque experience.

Navigating the canals of Venice is an unforgettable part of visiting the city. Whether you choose the public Vaporetto, a private gondola ride, or an adventurous kayak journey, each method offers its own charm and perspective. The canals are not just a means of transport but a window into the soul of Venice, providing insights into its beauty, history, and everyday life.

CHAPTER 4.
WHERE TO STAY
Hotels

Understanding the variety of hotel options in Venice can greatly enhance your stay, whether you're looking for a luxurious experience or a more budget-friendly choice. Here's a detailed look at some notable hotels in Venice and Mestre, with practical tips on how to enjoy your stay.

Rialto Unique Venice Experience offers a truly memorable stay right in the heart of Venice. Located at Sestiere San Polo, 315, Venice, Italy, this hotel is just a short walk from the famous Rialto Bridge. The building's charming architecture and unique Venetian décor provide an authentic atmosphere. From here, you can easily explore nearby attractions like the Grand Canal and Piazza San Marco. To get there, simply take a Vaporetto water bus to the Rialto stop, which is conveniently close. For budget travelers, booking in advance can help you secure better rates, and exploring local eateries instead of dining in tourist spots can keep costs down while offering an authentic taste of Venetian cuisine.

MEININGER Venezia Mestre, situated at Via Ca' Marcello, 19, Mestre, Italy, is a great option for those seeking comfort without breaking the bank. This hotel is located in Mestre, a short train ride away from Venice's main islands. The location offers easy access to Venice via the frequent train service that takes you to the Santa Lucia station in about 10 minutes. MEININGER provides modern amenities and is ideal for budget-conscious travelers. The hotel's communal areas and kitchen facilities make it easy to prepare your own meals, further saving on expenses. It's also well-situated for exploring Mestre, where you'll find local markets and restaurants.

Hotel Mercurio Venice is a charming and mid-range option located at Calle dei Fabbri, 4696, Venice, Italy. Situated near Piazza San Marco, this hotel puts you in close proximity to major attractions. The walk from the hotel to the square is picturesque, taking you through some of Venice's most beautiful streets and canals. To reach Hotel Mercurio, you can take the Vaporetto to the San Marco stop and walk a short distance. The hotel itself offers a warm atmosphere and personal service. To save money, consider taking advantage of their breakfast options and plan your sightseeing around free or low-cost attractions.

Hotel Ariston, located at Piazzale Santa Maria Elisabetta, 1, Lido di Venezia, Italy, is an excellent choice if you're looking for a quieter area with easy access to Venice's main attractions. Situated on the Lido island, this hotel provides a more relaxed environment away from the hustle and bustle of central Venice. You can reach Venice's main islands by taking a Vaporetto from the Lido to various stops in Venice. The hotel offers comfortable accommodations and a pleasant garden where you can unwind after a day of exploring. For budget-conscious travelers, the Lido offers a variety of reasonably priced dining options, and you can save on transportation costs by staying on the Lido and using the Vaporetto service to commute.

Leonardo Royal Hotel Venice Mestre, located at Via Ca' Marcello, 19, Mestre, Italy, offers modern comfort in Mestre, which is a good base for exploring Venice. This hotel is conveniently close to the train station, making it easy to commute to Venice. The rooms are well-equipped, and the hotel features amenities such as a fitness center and a restaurant. From the hotel, a quick train ride will take you to Venice's main attractions. For budget travelers, booking early and considering packages with breakfast included can help manage costs. Additionally, exploring Mestre's local dining options can provide good value for money.

Each of these hotels offers a unique experience in Venice and Mestre, catering to different preferences and budgets. When choosing your accommodation, consider what aspects of your trip are most important—whether it's proximity to attractions, comfort, or cost. Booking in advance, exploring local dining options, and using public transportation efficiently are key strategies for making the most of your stay while staying within budget.

Budget-Friendly Options

When traveling to Venice on a budget, finding comfortable yet affordable accommodation can enhance your experience without straining your wallet. Here are three budget-friendly options that offer great value, each with its unique charm and convenience.

Ducale Hotel is a fantastic choice for those looking for a budget-friendly yet comfortable stay. Located at Rio Terà San Leonardo, 152, Venice, Italy, this hotel is in a central area, making it easy to explore the city's key attractions. From Ducale Hotel, you can walk to the nearby Grand Canal and Rialto Bridge, which are just a short stroll away. To get there, take the Vaporetto water bus to the San Marcuola stop, which is close to the hotel. The Ducale Hotel provides simple but clean rooms, and the staff is known for being helpful and friendly. To make the most of your stay, explore local trattorias for affordable dining and consider buying a Vaporetto pass to save on transportation costs. Staying here allows you to experience Venice's vibrant atmosphere without overspending.

Hotel Agli Artisti, situated at Lista di Spagna, 230, Venice, Italy, offers another great budget-friendly option. This hotel is conveniently located near the Santa Lucia train station, making it an ideal choice for those arriving by train. From Hotel Agli Artisti, you can easily walk to the nearby Grand Canal and hop on Vaporetto lines to explore further. The rooms are modest but comfortable, providing a good base for sightseeing. To reach the hotel, simply follow the signs from the train station or take a short Vaporetto ride to the nearby

Ferrovia stop. For budget travelers, Hotel Agli Artisti's proximity to the train station and affordable rates make it a practical choice. Explore the surrounding neighborhood for inexpensive dining options and take advantage of the hotel's central location to navigate Venice's main attractions efficiently.

Giramondo B&B Venice is a charming and budget-friendly bed and breakfast located at Via Trevisan, 6, Mestre, Italy. Although it's situated in Mestre rather than central Venice, it's well connected with frequent train services to the city. The B&B offers a cozy atmosphere and a more homey feel compared to larger hotels. To get to Venice from Giramondo B&B, simply take a train from Mestre to Venice Santa Lucia station, which takes about 10 minutes. The B&B provides a hearty breakfast, which helps save on dining costs during the day. To enjoy Venice on a budget, use the time saved on commuting to explore Mestre's local markets and eateries for affordable meals. Staying in Mestre can be a cost-effective option, especially for longer stays, while still offering easy access to Venice's main attractions.

Each of these options provides a comfortable and affordable stay while allowing you to enjoy all that Venice has to offer. By choosing budget-friendly accommodations and exploring local dining options, you can make the most of your trip without exceeding your budget. Be sure to book in advance to secure the best rates and take advantage of Venice's public transportation system to explore the city efficiently.

Luxury Stays in Venice

For those seeking a luxurious stay in Venice, these five high-end accommodations offer exceptional comfort and elegance. Here's a detailed look at each, including addresses, transportation tips, and suggestions on how to make the most of your stay.

Hilton Molino Stucky Venice, located at Giudecca 810, Venice, Italy, is a grand and historic hotel that combines modern luxury with stunning architecture. Set in a converted flour mill on the Giudecca Island, the Hilton Molino Stucky offers breathtaking views of Venice's skyline and the lagoon. To get there, take Vaporetto line 2 from the main islands to the Giudecca stop, and then a short walk will lead you to the hotel. The Hilton Molino Stucky boasts a rooftop bar with panoramic views, a luxurious spa, and an impressive swimming pool. To make the most of your stay, enjoy a cocktail at the rooftop bar during sunset and explore the nearby Giudecca Island for a more tranquil side of Venice. Although it's a splurge, the experience is worth every penny for those wanting to indulge in Venice's grandeur.

Villa Giotto Luxury Suite & Apartments, found at Campo San Polo, 2651, Venice, Italy, provides a unique blend of luxury and privacy. Located in the heart of Venice's San Polo district, this accommodation offers spacious suites and apartments with elegant décor and modern amenities. To reach Villa Giotto, take Vaporetto line 1 to the San Silvestro stop, which is a short walk away. The property's central location allows easy access to key attractions like the Rialto Bridge and the Grand Canal. For a memorable experience, enjoy a leisurely stroll through the San Polo district's charming streets and discover its local markets and restaurants. The luxury and independence of staying in a well-appointed apartment make it ideal for longer stays or those seeking a more home-like atmosphere.

The Venice Venice Hotel, situated at Rio Tera' dei Pensieri, 3764, Venice, Italy, is a modern and stylish luxury option in the heart of Venice. This hotel features contemporary design and offers comfortable, high-end rooms. To get there, take Vaporetto line 1 or 2 to the Rialto stop, and it's a short walk from there. The Venice Venice Hotel provides excellent amenities, including a chic lounge and bar. For a special experience, enjoy a private gondola ride or a fine dining experience at a nearby restaurant. The hotel's central location means you can easily explore Venice's main attractions, including St. Mark's Basilica and the Doge's Palace, all within walking distance.

Ca' Sagredo Hotel, located at Campo Santa Sofia, 4198, Venice, Italy, is a historic gem offering a unique blend of luxury and history. Housed in a 15th-century palace, this hotel features elegant rooms with classic Venetian décor and stunning views of the Grand Canal. To reach Ca' Sagredo Hotel, take Vaporetto line 1 to the Ca' d'Oro stop, and the hotel is a short walk away. Enjoy the hotel's rich history and magnificent interiors, and take time to relax in the opulent surroundings. For a touch of local flavor, explore the nearby Rialto Market and enjoy Venetian cuisine at nearby trattorias. The Ca' Sagredo Hotel provides an immersive experience in Venice's rich cultural heritage.

Hotel Danieli, Venice, located at Riva degli Schiavoni, 4196, Venice, Italy, is renowned for its opulent luxury and historical significance. This iconic hotel offers magnificent views of St. Mark's Basin and is known for its lavish rooms and exquisite dining options. To get there, take Vaporetto line 1 to the San Zaccaria stop, and it's a short walk from there. The Hotel Danieli's location is perfect for exploring nearby landmarks such as St. Mark's Basilica and the Doge's Palace. For a truly memorable experience, dine at the hotel's restaurant, which offers fine Venetian cuisine with a view. The grandeur of the Hotel Danieli makes it a top choice for those seeking a luxurious and unforgettable stay in Venice.

Each of these luxury accommodations provides a distinctive Venetian experience with exceptional service and comfort. While they may come with a higher price tag, the luxurious amenities and prime locations make them worthwhile for those looking to indulge in the best of Venice. For travelers on a budget, consider exploring special offers or off-season rates to enjoy a touch of luxury without breaking the bank.

Staying on the Islands: Murano, Burano, and Beyond

Staying on the islands of Venice offers a unique perspective of the city beyond the bustling main areas. Murano, Burano, and Torcello each provide distinct experiences that highlight different aspects of Venetian culture and charm.

Murano, famous for its glassmaking, is a must-visit for anyone interested in artisan crafts. The island's address is Murano, 30141 Venice, Italy. To reach Murano, take Vaporetto line 4.1 or 4.2 from Venice's main islands to Murano Faro or Murano Colonna stops. Wandering through Murano, you'll find numerous glass workshops where you can witness traditional glassblowing techniques and even purchase beautiful handcrafted pieces. Visit the Murano Glass Museum, located at Museo del Vetro, Piazza San Pietro Martire, 1, to delve into the island's rich history of glassmaking. For a more budget-friendly experience, look for smaller, less touristy shops where you can find unique glass items at lower prices.

Burano is known for its brightly colored houses and lace-making tradition. Its address is Burano, 30142 Venice, Italy. To get to Burano, take Vaporetto line 12 from Venice's main islands to the Burano stop. Once there, enjoy a leisurely walk through its picturesque streets, where the vivid colors of the houses create a vibrant and photogenic scene. The lace museum, located at Museo del Merletto, Piazza Baldassarre Galuppi, 187, showcases the intricate lacework that Burano is renowned for. To fully enjoy Burano's charm, consider dining at a local trattoria where you can savor fresh seafood dishes, often at more reasonable prices compared to central Venice.

Torcello, the least developed of the three, offers a peaceful retreat and a glimpse into Venice's past. The address is Torcello, 30142 Venice, Italy. To reach Torcello, take Vaporetto line 12 from Venice to the Torcello stop. The island is known for its historical sites, including the Basilica di Santa Maria Assunta, which features stunning Byzantine mosaics. Explore the tranquil surroundings, including the picturesque landscape and the small but charming Torcello Museum. For a budget-friendly visit, bring a picnic to enjoy in the island's serene setting, as dining options are limited and can be pricey.

When planning a stay on these islands, consider their unique atmospheres and how they align with your interests. Murano's artistic vibe, Burano's colorful streets, and Torcello's historical allure offer varied experiences that can enrich your visit to Venice. Each island has its own charm and is well worth exploring if you want to escape the crowds and discover a different side of Venice.

For travelers on a budget, staying on these islands can often be more affordable than central Venice, though it's important to book accommodations early to secure the best rates. Enjoying local eateries and shopping directly from artisans can also help you manage costs while making the most of your Venetian island adventure.

CHAPTER 5.
GUIDE TO VENICE'S NEIGHBORHOOD
San Marco

San Marco is the heart of Venice and undoubtedly one of its most iconic areas. The grand square, known as Piazza San Marco, is a must-visit for anyone exploring this enchanting city.

To get to San Marco, you can take Vaporetto line 1 or 2 from various stops along the Grand Canal directly to the San Marco stop. If you're coming from the train station or bus terminal in Piazzale Roma, Vaporetto lines 1 or 2 are also convenient options. Alternatively, you can walk from many central locations, but be prepared for some winding streets and plenty of crowds.

At the center of San Marco is the magnificent Basilica di San Marco, or St. Mark's Basilica. Located at Piazza San Marco, 328, Venice, this stunning cathedral is renowned for its Byzantine architecture and intricate mosaics. The interior is nothing short of breathtaking, with golden mosaics and elaborate designs that reflect centuries of artistic and architectural mastery. Make sure to take a moment to admire the Pala d'Oro, a golden altarpiece encrusted with gems.

Adjacent to the basilica is the Campanile di San Marco, the bell tower offering sweeping views of Venice. Climbing to the top is well worth it for a panoramic view of the city and its surrounding lagoon. The tower is located in Piazza San Marco, and tickets can be purchased on-site.

Another highlight in the area is the Doge's Palace, or Palazzo Ducale, situated right next to the basilica at Piazza San Marco, 1. This historic building was the residence of the Doge, the chief magistrate of Venice, and serves as a museum today. The opulent rooms and the famous Bridge of Sighs, which connects the palace to the old prison, offer a fascinating glimpse into Venice's political and judicial history.

For a unique perspective of San Marco, consider a gondola ride along the canals that surround the square. Although gondola rides can be on the pricier side, they offer an unforgettable experience and a different view of the city's architectural beauty.

While you're in the area, don't miss the chance to relax at one of the many cafes lining Piazza San Marco. Grab a coffee or gelato and soak in the lively atmosphere. Be aware that prices at these cafes can be higher due to the prime location, but the experience of sitting in the heart of Venice with a view of the square is quite special.

For a taste of local Venetian life and a break from the crowds, explore the nearby streets and smaller squares. The shops and restaurants here offer a range of options from casual dining to upscale cuisine, often with fewer tourists than those directly in Piazza San Marco.

San Marco is a vibrant and essential part of Venice, offering a wealth of history, culture, and beautiful sights. Whether you're marveling at the architecture, enjoying the views from the Campanile, or simply wandering through the lively square, this area provides an unforgettable Venetian experience.

Cannaregio

Cannaregio is one of Venice's most charming and vibrant neighborhoods, offering a more local and authentic experience compared to the heavily touristed areas. Located in the northern part of the city, Cannaregio provides a fascinating glimpse into everyday Venetian life and is home to a rich tapestry of history and culture.

To get to Cannaregio, you can take Vaporetto lines 4.1 or 4.2, which stop at the Fondamenta Nuove station. If you're coming from the central train station, Santa Lucia, it's a pleasant walk through winding streets, or you can hop on Vaporetto line 1, which also makes stops along the Grand Canal before heading to Cannaregio.

A highlight of Cannaregio is the Ghetto Ebraico, or the Jewish Ghetto, located around Campo del Ghetto Nuovo. This area, at Campo del Ghetto Nuovo, 30121 Venice, is the historic heart of Venice's Jewish community. The Ghetto is a poignant reminder of Venice's history and is home to several historic synagogues and a small Jewish Museum. Exploring this area offers a unique perspective on the city's diverse past. The Ghetto itself is an atmospheric place with narrow streets and charming squares. The synagogues are still active, and visiting them provides insight into the community's rich heritage.

Not far from the Ghetto is the beautiful Church of Santa Maria dei Miracoli, located at Campo Santa Maria dei Miracoli, 30121 Venice. This church is a hidden gem of Venetian architecture, renowned for its intricate marble façade and stunning interior. It's a peaceful place to visit, offering a serene break from the busier parts of the city.

Cannaregio also boasts a lively atmosphere in its smaller squares and canals. One particularly lovely spot is the Strada Nuova, a main street running through the neighborhood. Here, you'll find a variety of shops, cafes, and local eateries. It's a great place to enjoy a coffee or a meal and observe daily Venetian life. The area around Campo Santa Margherita is also vibrant, known for its bustling market and lively evening atmosphere. This square, located at Campo Santa Margherita, 30123 Venice, is a popular spot among locals and students from the nearby university.

For a delightful stroll, wander along the canals and discover the picturesque bridges and charming facades of Cannaregio. The neighborhood is known for its beautiful, colorful buildings and peaceful waterways, offering plenty of photo opportunities. The Fondamenta della Misericordia and Fondamenta dei Ormesini are particularly scenic stretches along the canals, lined with traditional Venetian architecture and small local businesses.

Dining in Cannaregio offers a range of experiences, from casual trattorias to more refined restaurants. For a taste of local Venetian cuisine, try a traditional osteria such as Osteria Al Bacco at Fondamenta della Misericordia, 30121 Venice. It's a great place to sample dishes like cicchetti (Venetian tapas) and fresh seafood in a relaxed setting.

Cannaregio is a neighborhood that beautifully combines history, culture, and everyday Venetian life. Whether you're exploring its historic sites, strolling along the canals, or enjoying a meal in one of its local eateries, Cannaregio provides a rich and authentic Venetian experience.

Dorsoduro

Dorsoduro is a delightful neighborhood in Venice, known for its artistic vibe and peaceful atmosphere. Located on the southern part of the city, it's one of the more tranquil areas, offering a pleasant escape from the bustling crowds of more central districts.

To get to Dorsoduro, you can take Vaporetto line 1, which stops at the Accademia or Salute stations, depending on where you want to start your exploration. If you're arriving from the main train station, Santa Lucia, it's a lovely walk across the Accademia Bridge, which offers beautiful views of the Grand Canal.

One of the first places to visit in Dorsoduro is the Gallerie dell'Accademia, located at Campo della Carità, 1050, 30123 Venice. This renowned museum houses an extensive collection of Venetian art from the Middle Ages to the Renaissance. It's a fantastic place to see masterpieces by artists like Titian, Veronese, and Bellini. The museum's peaceful atmosphere allows you to appreciate the art without the usual crowds found in other parts of the city.

Another must-see is the Peggy Guggenheim Collection, situated at Palazzo Venier dei Leoni, Dorsoduro 701, 30123 Venice. This museum, once the home of the American art collector Peggy Guggenheim, features an impressive collection of modern art, including works by Picasso, Pollock, and Kandinsky. The museum's setting, overlooking the Grand Canal, is as enchanting as the artwork inside.

For a charming Venetian experience, head to the Church of Santa Maria della Salute, located at Campo Santa Maria della

Salute, 30123 Venice. This iconic baroque church, with its distinctive dome, is not only an architectural marvel but also offers breathtaking views of the Grand Canal from its steps. It's a wonderful spot to take a moment and enjoy the serene surroundings.

Dorsoduro is also home to the vibrant Campo Santa Margherita, located at Campo Santa Margherita, 30123 Venice. This lively square is a hub of local activity, especially in the evenings when locals gather for drinks and socializing. It's a great place to experience the everyday life of Venetians and enjoy a casual meal or coffee at one of the many nearby cafes and restaurants.

The neighborhood's canals are also worth exploring. Take a leisurely walk along the Fondamenta delle Zattere, a long promenade that runs along the southern edge of Dorsoduro. Here, you can enjoy stunning views of the Giudecca Canal and the islands beyond. The promenade is perfect for a relaxed stroll, and you'll find plenty of gelato shops and cafes where you can stop for a treat.

For a more authentic Venetian experience, consider visiting the traditional artisan shops and studios scattered throughout Dorsoduro. The neighborhood is known for its crafts, including glassblowing and mask-making. It's a great opportunity to see artisans at work and perhaps purchase a unique souvenir.

Dorsoduro offers a more laid-back and artistic side of Venice. Whether you're admiring art in one of its museums, enjoying a stroll along its canals, or soaking in the local atmosphere at a lively square, the neighborhood provides a rich and enjoyable experience.

Castello

Castello is one of Venice's largest and most intriguing neighborhoods, offering a blend of historic charm and local life. It's located on the eastern side of the city, stretching from the Grand Canal to the edge of the lagoon, making it a fascinating area to explore.

To get to Castello, you can take Vaporetto line 1 or 5.1 to the Arsenale stop, which is a convenient entry point to the neighborhood. If you're coming from the main train station, Santa Lucia, a pleasant walk will take you across the famous Ponte di Rialto and along the quieter streets of Castello.

One of the highlights of Castello is the Venetian Arsenal, located at Campo della Tana, 30122 Venice. This historical complex was once a bustling shipyard and naval base and played a crucial role in Venice's maritime dominance. Although you can't enter all areas, the exterior is impressive, and you can learn about its history from the nearby Museo Storico Navale (Naval Historical Museum), located at Arsenale di Venezia, 30122 Venice. The museum houses a collection of maritime artifacts and models that provide insight into Venice's naval history.

Just a short walk from the Arsenal is the beautiful Church of San Pietro di Castello, located at Campo San Pietro, 30122 Venice. This church, which once served as the cathedral of Venice before St. Mark's, is less crowded than other churches and offers a peaceful place to reflect. Its interior features lovely frescoes and a serene atmosphere, making it a great spot to appreciate Venice's religious art and history.

For a taste of local life, visit the lively Campo Santa Maria Formosa, located at Campo Santa Maria Formosa, 30122 Venice. This bustling square is surrounded by cafes and shops, providing a perfect spot to sit and people-watch. The square is also home to the Church of Santa Maria Formosa, which, while less well-known, boasts a beautiful facade and a rich history.

Another gem in Castello is the vibrant Via Garibaldi, a street known for its local shops and eateries. Located at Via Garibaldi, 30122 Venice, it offers a more authentic Venetian experience compared to the tourist-heavy areas. Here, you can find charming boutiques, bakeries, and traditional restaurants. It's an excellent place to sample local Venetian cuisine and enjoy a leisurely meal.

Castello is also home to the serene Giardini Pubblici, located at Viale Giuseppe Garibaldi, 30122 Venice. This public garden provides a green escape from the city's hustle and bustle. It's a lovely place for a relaxing stroll, with paths shaded by trees and views of the lagoon.

Exploring Castello offers a blend of historical exploration and local charm. Whether you're wandering through its historic sites, relaxing in its gardens, or enjoying the local vibe in its squares and streets, Castello provides a rich and varied experience of Venice.

Santa Croce

Santa Croce is one of Venice's six historic neighborhoods, situated in the western part of the city, along the Grand Canal. It's a less touristy area compared to some of the more famous parts of Venice, making it a great place to explore if you want to experience the city like a local.

To reach Santa Croce, you can hop on Vaporetto line 1 or 2 and get off at the San Stae stop. Alternatively, if you're coming from the Santa Lucia train station, it's just a short walk across the bridge over the Grand Canal.

One of the key attractions in Santa Croce is the Church of San Stae, located at Campo San Stae, 30135 Venice. This church, known for its beautiful Baroque facade, is a stunning example of Venetian architecture. The interior is equally impressive, featuring a collection of works by famous Venetian artists. It's a peaceful place to visit and less crowded compared to other churches in Venice.

Another must-see is the Ca' Pesaro, situated at Santa Croce, 2076, 30135 Venice. This stunning Baroque palace houses the International Gallery of Modern Art and the Museum of Oriental Art. The museum's collection includes works by 20th-century artists and an impressive array of Asian art. The building itself is worth a visit, with its ornate design and lovely views over the Grand Canal.

For a taste of local Venetian life, wander through the Campo San Giacomo dell'Orio, located at Campo San Giacomo dell'Orio, 30135 Venice. This lively square is surrounded by cafes and local shops, making it a great spot to sit down and enjoy a coffee or a meal. The square features a beautiful church, San Giacomo dell'Orio, which is known for its simple yet charming architecture and its tranquil ambiance.

Santa Croce is also home to the vibrant Mercato di Rialto, located at the Rialto Bridge area, just a short walk from Santa Croce. This bustling market is a fantastic place to explore, offering a wide range of fresh produce, seafood, and local specialties. It's a great spot to pick up some unique ingredients or just to soak in the lively atmosphere.

Another highlight is the Museo di Storia Naturale, located at Santa Croce, 1730, 30135 Venice. This Natural History Museum offers a fascinating collection of exhibits ranging from fossils to taxidermied animals. It's a great place to learn more about the natural world and is a fun visit for families and anyone interested in science.

Santa Croce is also known for its charming streets and canals. Take some time to wander through the neighborhood's narrow alleys and discover its hidden corners. You'll find picturesque canals, quaint bridges, and traditional Venetian houses that offer a glimpse into everyday life in Venice.

In Santa Croce, you can enjoy a more relaxed and authentic Venetian experience. Whether you're visiting historical sites, exploring local markets, or simply strolling through the neighborhood, Santa Croce provides a unique and enriching way to experience Venice.

San Polo

San Polo is one of Venice's historic and vibrant districts, nestled between the Grand Canal and the Rialto Bridge. It's a lively area known for its bustling markets, charming squares, and historic sites, offering a great glimpse into both the past and present of Venice.

To get to San Polo, you can take Vaporetto line 1 or 2 and disembark at the Rialto stop. From there, it's just a short walk to the heart of the neighborhood. Alternatively, if you're coming from the Santa Lucia train station, you can walk directly to San Polo, crossing the Grand Canal via the Rialto Bridge.

One of the most notable landmarks in San Polo is the Rialto Market, located around the Rialto Bridge. The market, situated at the intersection of the Ruga degli Orefici and the Ruga Vecchia, is a vibrant place to explore. The food market is known for its fresh seafood, fruits, and vegetables, offering a sensory feast of colors and aromas. It's a fantastic spot to soak up the local atmosphere and perhaps pick up some ingredients if you're planning to cook.

Just a short distance from the market, you'll find the beautiful Church of San Giacomo di Rialto, located at Campo San Giacomo di Rialto, 30125 Venice. This church is one of the oldest in Venice, dating back to the 9th century. It's renowned for its simple yet elegant façade and its serene, peaceful interior. The church's location near the market makes it a convenient stop during your exploration of the area.

San Polo is also home to the Scuola Grande di San Rocco, situated at Campo San Rocco, 30125 Venice. This historical building is famous for its impressive collection of paintings by Tintoretto. The interior is adorned with his masterpieces, making it a must-visit for art enthusiasts. The grandeur of the building and the beauty of the artwork make it a memorable stop.

For a taste of local Venetian life, head to Campo San Polo, located at Campo San Polo, 30125 Venice. This large square is one of the biggest in Venice and is surrounded by traditional Venetian buildings and lively cafes. It's a perfect spot to sit down, enjoy a coffee, and watch the world go by. The square often hosts local events and festivals, adding to its vibrant atmosphere.

Another interesting spot in San Polo is the Palazzo Pesaro, situated at Santa Croce, 2076, 30135 Venice. This grand palace now houses the International Gallery of Modern Art. The museum offers an eclectic collection of modern art and provides an interesting contrast to the historical sites of Venice.

San Polo is also known for its narrow streets and charming canals. Take some time to wander through the labyrinth of alleyways and discover hidden gems such as quaint shops, traditional Venetian cafes, and picturesque canal views. The area's more relaxed pace compared to other parts of Venice allows for a more intimate and enjoyable exploration.

Whether you're visiting historic sites, exploring local markets, or simply soaking in the atmosphere of the charming streets and squares, San Polo offers a rich and rewarding experience for anyone looking to delve deeper into the heart of Venice.

CHAPTER 6.
TOP ATTRACTIONS
St. Mark's Basilica

St. Mark's Basilica is truly the jewel of Venice, a stunning masterpiece that captures the city's rich history and opulence. Situated in the heart of Venice at Piazza San Marco, 30124 Venice, it's impossible to miss this majestic cathedral as it stands prominently against the backdrop of the square. To get there, you can either take Vaporetto line 1 or 2 and disembark at the San Marco stop, which places you just a short walk away from the basilica, or if you're already exploring the city on foot, it's a central landmark that's easy to locate.

My visit to St. Mark's Basilica was nothing short of awe-inspiring. As I approached the basilica, its intricate façade, adorned with golden mosaics and delicate marble carvings, immediately captured my attention. The grandeur of the entrance, flanked by the four bronze horses, set the tone for the magnificence that awaited inside.

Upon entering the basilica, I was struck by the breathtaking interior. The entire ceiling and walls are covered in shimmering mosaics that depict biblical scenes and historical events in vibrant colors and gold. The floor, with its intricate patterns, is equally mesmerizing. The sheer scale and beauty of the mosaics create an atmosphere of awe and reverence.

To make the most of your visit, it's a good idea to take a moment to simply stand in the middle of the basilica and take in the grandeur. If you're interested in learning more about the history and significance of the basilica, audio guides are available for rent. They offer fascinating insights into the basilica's art, architecture, and historical context.

One of the highlights of my visit was the chance to see the Pala d'Oro, an ornate altarpiece adorned with precious gems and intricate gold work. It's displayed in the basilica's high altar and is a testament to the wealth and artistic prowess of Venice during its heyday. Make sure to check the opening hours of the basilica's museum and treasury, as they house other important artifacts and artworks that are worth seeing.

The entrance to St. Mark's Basilica is free, though there are additional fees if you want to access certain areas like the museum or the terraces. I found that visiting early in the morning or later in the afternoon helped avoid the largest crowds, making the experience more enjoyable and serene. Also, dress modestly as a sign of respect, as the basilica is a place of worship.

If you're visiting during peak tourist seasons, consider booking a skip-the-line ticket in advance to avoid long queues. The basilica can get quite busy, especially during summer months, so having a reserved time slot can save you time and make your visit smoother.

Aside from exploring the interior, spending some time outside in Piazza San Marco is also worthwhile. The square is bustling with activity and offers fantastic views of the basilica's façade. You can sit at one of the many cafes surrounding the square, enjoy a coffee, and take in the vibrant atmosphere.

St. Mark's Basilica is not just a place of historical and artistic significance; it's also a symbol of Venice's rich cultural heritage. Visiting this incredible cathedral offers a profound experience that reflects the beauty and grandeur of Venice, leaving you with lasting memories of this extraordinary city.

Doge's Palace

Visiting Doge's Palace, or Palazzo Ducale, is like stepping into a grand chapter of Venice's rich history. Situated at Piazza San Marco, 1, 30124 Venice, it commands attention with its striking Gothic architecture and the elaborate façade that reflects the city's former glory.

To reach the palace, you can easily hop off at the San Marco Vaporetto stop, which is conveniently close. If you're navigating Venice by foot, the palace is a short stroll from St. Mark's Basilica and is a key feature of the square, so it's hard to miss.

When I visited Doge's Palace, the first thing that struck me was its magnificent entrance. The palace's façade, adorned with intricate carvings and delicate arches, immediately sets the stage for the opulence inside. As you step through the grand entrance, you're greeted by a sense of awe at the sheer scale and historical significance of the place.

The interior of Doge's Palace is a treasure trove of Venetian art and history. The grand halls, with their ornate ceilings and grandiose décor, speak volumes about the city's wealth and power during the height of the Venetian Republic. The Hall of the Great Council, in particular, is a highlight with its stunning frescoes and elaborate decor that showcases the artistry of the period.

One of the most intriguing parts of the palace is the Secret Itineraries tour. This tour takes you through hidden rooms and passages that were once used for secret meetings and political intrigue. It provides a fascinating glimpse into the inner workings of Venetian governance and the intriguing history of the Doges. Be sure to book this tour in advance as it's incredibly popular and can offer a unique perspective on Venetian history.

The palace also houses the impressive Bridge of Sighs, which you can view from within. This bridge connects the palace to the old prison and is named for the sighs of prisoners who would have crossed it on their way to incarceration. Seeing it up close adds a poignant layer to the history of the palace.

Admission to Doge's Palace is not free, but the entrance fee is well worth it for the chance to explore such an iconic landmark. It's advisable to purchase tickets ahead of time, especially during peak tourist seasons, to avoid long lines. Tickets grant you access to the palace's main rooms and the Museo dell'Opera, where you can see various artworks and historical artifacts.

To make the most of your visit, consider using an audio guide or joining a guided tour. These options provide in-depth information and context that enrich the experience, allowing you to appreciate the historical and artistic significance of each room and exhibit.

Spending a few hours at Doge's Palace is a rewarding experience. After exploring the grand halls and secret rooms, you can relax in the surrounding Piazza San Marco. The area is lively and perfect for people-watching, and you can enjoy a coffee at one of the nearby cafes while taking in the view of the palace's impressive façade.

Doge's Palace is a must-see when in Venice. Its grandeur, historical depth, and artistic treasures offer an unforgettable experience that brings Venice's rich past to life.

Rialto Bridge and Market

Exploring the Rialto Bridge and Market is a highlight of any trip to Venice, offering a vibrant slice of Venetian life. The Rialto Bridge, known as Ponte di Rialto, is one of the city's most famous landmarks and a beautiful piece of Renaissance architecture. Located at the intersection of the Grand Canal and the Mercato area, it's easy to find at the address of Riva del Ferro, 30125 Venice.

Getting to the Rialto Bridge is straightforward. If you're traveling by Vaporetto, the Rialto stop places you right in the heart of the action. Alternatively, if you're strolling through Venice, the bridge is a central point, and walking there will let you soak in the city's charming streets and canals.

When I visited the Rialto Bridge, I was struck by its elegance. The bridge arches gracefully over the Grand Canal, offering stunning views of the bustling waterway below. The bridge itself is lined with shops, making it a lively spot where you can pick up Venetian souvenirs or simply enjoy the atmosphere. Standing on the bridge, I admired the view of the colorful buildings and the boats gliding along the canal, making it a perfect photo opportunity.

As for the Rialto Market, located just a short walk from the bridge, it's a sensory feast. The market is housed in a vibrant square, and as you approach, you're greeted by the lively hum of vendors and the aroma of fresh produce and seafood. The market is divided into two main sections: the fish market and the produce market.

The fish market, known as the Mercato del Pesce, is where you'll find an impressive array of seafood. The stalls are brimming with everything from fresh fish to clams and octopus. Watching the vendors interact with locals and tourists alike provides a glimpse into daily Venetian life and the city's culinary culture.

Nearby, the produce market, or Mercato della Frutta e Verdura, offers a colorful display of fruits and vegetables. The vibrant colors and the sheer variety of produce make it a delightful place to wander through. Even if you're not buying, the market is worth a visit just to experience the bustling atmosphere and see the local produce.

Both the Rialto Bridge and Market are free to visit, though you might want to budget for any purchases you make at the market. To fully enjoy your time, I recommend visiting in the morning when the market is at its busiest and the vendors are most active. Early mornings are also cooler, making it a pleasant time to explore before the crowds arrive.

If you're interested in history, the Rialto Bridge offers more than just picturesque views. It has been a vital part of Venice's trade and commerce since the late 16th century, and walking across it feels like stepping into a living piece of history.

For a deeper dive into the area, consider taking a walking tour that includes the Rialto Bridge and Market. Many tours provide additional insights into the history and significance of these landmarks, enhancing your understanding of their place in Venetian culture.

A visit to the Rialto Bridge and Market provides a wonderful blend of scenic beauty and local flavor. From the architectural splendor of the bridge to the vibrant hustle and bustle of the market, it's an experience that captures the essence of Venice in a uniquely engaging way.

Grand Canal: The Heart of Venice

The Grand Canal is truly the heart of Venice, offering an unforgettable glimpse into the city's unique charm and vibrant life. This main waterway winds its way through the center of Venice, stretching about 3.8 kilometers and showcasing the city's stunning architecture and bustling activity.

To get to the Grand Canal, you'll find that it's a central part of Venice, so it's quite easy to reach from various parts of the city. The main addresses along the canal include the Fondamenta Nove, 30121 Venice, and the Rialto Bridge, located at Riva del Ferro, 30125 Venice. If you're traveling by Vaporetto, there are several stops along the canal including the Grand Canal Stop, which is perfectly situated for accessing key points along the waterway.

During my visit to the Grand Canal, I was struck by the sheer beauty of the scene. The canal is flanked by majestic buildings, some of which date back to the Renaissance and Gothic periods. As I floated along the canal on a Vaporetto, I felt like I was gliding through a living museum, with each turn offering a new perspective on the city's rich history. The buildings that line the canal, with their ornate facades and colorful exteriors, create a stunning backdrop against the shimmering water.

One of the best ways to experience the Grand Canal is to take a Vaporetto ride. The Vaporetto is Venice's public water bus service, and it offers a relaxed and scenic way to see the city. The journey provides an overview of the Grand Canal, allowing you to marvel at the architecture and observe the daily hustle of Venetian life. The ride is affordable and a must-do, especially if you're new to Venice. You can catch the Vaporetto at various stops along the canal, including at the main terminal points such as Piazzale Roma and the train station.

For a more intimate experience, consider taking a gondola ride. Although gondola rides are more expensive than the Vaporetto, they offer a unique perspective of the Grand Canal and its surrounding areas. As I drifted along the canal in a gondola, I enjoyed the quiet serenity and the chance to see the city from a more personal angle. The gondoliers often provide interesting anecdotes and historical insights about the buildings and landmarks you pass.

Another fantastic way to enjoy the Grand Canal is to simply wander along its banks. The areas around the canal are dotted with charming shops, cafes, and restaurants. I found that exploring on foot allowed me to discover hidden gems, from quaint cafes where I could enjoy a coffee with a view to small artisan shops selling unique souvenirs. The bustling Rialto Market, located near the bridge of the same name, is a lively spot worth exploring for its fresh produce and local specialties.

In terms of enjoying your time, try to visit the Grand Canal at different times of the day. The morning light offers beautiful reflections on the water and a quieter atmosphere, while the evening brings a vibrant energy as locals and tourists alike fill the area. The canal is free to visit, but if you plan on taking a Vaporetto or gondola ride, be prepared for the associated costs.

For a deeper dive into Venice's history, consider visiting some of the museums and landmarks situated along the Grand Canal. The Ca' d'Oro and the Peggy Guggenheim Collection are both excellent choices, offering insights into Venetian art and history.

The Grand Canal is the beating heart of Venice, offering a blend of architectural splendor and lively activity. Whether you choose to explore by Vaporetto, gondola, or on foot, you'll find that this iconic waterway provides a quintessential Venetian experience.

Gallerie dell'Accademia

Gallerie dell'Accademia, located at Campo della Carità, 1050, Venice, is a treasure trove of Venetian art, housed in a grand historical building. It's one of the city's most important art museums, showcasing a rich collection of masterpieces from the 14th to the 18th centuries.

To get to Gallerie dell'Accademia, I found that taking a Vaporetto along the Grand Canal was an excellent option. I alighted at the Accademia stop, which is conveniently close to the museum. If you're walking, the museum is also accessible from Piazzale Roma and the Santa Lucia train station, though it's a bit of a stroll through the charming, narrow streets of Venice.

The entrance to Gallerie dell'Accademia is paid, with ticket prices generally around 15 euros for adults. There are reduced prices for EU citizens aged 18-25 and free entry for children under 18. As I entered the museum, I was immediately struck by the stunning array of Venetian art that awaited inside. The museum is housed in an old convent and has an elegant, historic atmosphere that adds to the experience.

Inside, the collection is extensive and impressive. The galleries are divided by periods, showcasing works by famous Venetian artists like Titian, Tintoretto, and Veronese. I was particularly captivated by Titian's "Assumption of the Virgin" and Tintoretto's "The Last Supper." Walking through the rooms, each piece seemed to tell its own story of Venice's past, and I found myself lost in the detailed brushstrokes and vibrant colors of these masterpieces.

One of the highlights of my visit was the museum's collection of wooden altarpieces and the assortment of Renaissance and Baroque paintings. The museum also features a fine collection of sculptures and ancient manuscripts, giving visitors a comprehensive view of Venetian artistic heritage.

To fully appreciate your visit, I recommend taking a leisurely approach, allowing time to absorb each artwork. Audio guides are available and can provide additional context and details about the pieces on display, enriching the experience further. I opted for a guided tour, which offered fascinating insights and helped me understand the historical significance of many works.

For a break, there's a small café within the museum where you can grab a coffee or a light snack. It's a nice spot to sit and reflect on the art you've just seen. If you prefer to explore the surroundings, the museum is located in a picturesque area of

Venice. The nearby area offers beautiful canals and quaint streets that are perfect for a leisurely walk after your visit.

Gallerie dell'Accademia is a must-visit for anyone interested in art and Venetian history. It offers a deep dive into the city's artistic legacy, with a well-curated collection that highlights the grandeur of Venetian painting. With its central location and rich offerings, it's a cultural gem that enriches any visit to Venice.

Peggy Guggenheim Collection

The Peggy Guggenheim Collection is located at Dorsoduro, 701 - 30123 Venice. This museum is a highlight for anyone interested in modern art and offers a unique glimpse into Peggy Guggenheim's impressive private collection. To reach the museum, I took the Vaporetto along the Grand Canal and got off at the Accademia stop. From there, it was about a 15-minute walk through the charming streets of the Dorsoduro district.

The entrance to the Peggy Guggenheim Collection requires a ticket. As of my last visit, the ticket price was approximately 15 euros for adults. There are discounted rates for EU citizens aged 18-25 and free entry for children under 10. The museum also offers free admission on certain public holidays and the first Sunday of each month.

Upon arrival, I was greeted by the museum's elegant façade and its serene garden, which leads to the entrance. The museum is housed in Peggy Guggenheim's former home, a beautiful Venetian palace right on the Grand Canal. The setting itself adds a special charm to the experience.

Inside, the collection spans from the early 20th century to the mid-century, showcasing works by renowned artists like Jackson Pollock, Salvador Dalí, and Marc Chagall. The museum is divided into several rooms, each displaying a curated selection of Guggenheim's collection of modern art. I was particularly captivated by the abstract and surrealist pieces, which were vibrant and thought-provoking.

One of the highlights of my visit was the chance to see Pollock's "Mural" up close, along with Dalí's "The Birth of Liquid Desires." Each piece is thoughtfully displayed, allowing for a close examination of the details and the innovative techniques used by these groundbreaking artists.

The museum also features a lovely sculpture garden where you can take a relaxing break. The garden is a peaceful spot to sit and enjoy views of the Grand Canal, adding to the overall experience. There is a small café near the garden where you can grab a coffee or a light snack if needed.

For a more in-depth experience, I recommend taking advantage of the museum's audio guides or joining a guided tour. These provide valuable insights into the artworks and the history of Peggy Guggenheim's collection. The staff at the museum are knowledgeable and friendly, and they can offer additional information if you have any specific questions about the artworks or the collection.

The Peggy Guggenheim Collection is a must-visit for art enthusiasts and anyone interested in modern art. The museum's unique collection and beautiful setting make for a memorable visit. Whether you're an art lover or just looking for a culturally enriching experience in Venice, this museum offers a fascinating and enjoyable experience.

Teatro La Fenice

Teatro La Fenice, located at Campo San Fantin, 1965, 30124 Venice, is one of the most prestigious and historic opera houses in Italy. This iconic theater is renowned for its opulent interiors, rich history, and world-class performances. To get there, I used the Vaporetto and disembarked at the San Marco Vallaresso stop. From there, it was a short, pleasant walk through the charming streets of Venice to the theater.

The entrance to Teatro La Fenice typically requires a ticket. If you're interested in attending a performance, ticket prices vary based on the show and seating choice. For a more budget-friendly option, you might consider attending one of their daytime tours. As of my last visit, a standard tour cost around 10 euros, which provides a fascinating glimpse into the theater's history and architecture.

Upon arriving at La Fenice, I was struck by the grandeur of its façade. The building's ornate details and historical significance are evident from the moment you see it. The theater itself, which was originally opened in 1792, has been meticulously restored after being damaged by fire, and walking inside feels like stepping back in time.

The interior of Teatro La Fenice is nothing short of breathtaking. The opulent decoration includes gold leaf, exquisite chandeliers, and lush red velvet seating. During my visit, I joined a guided tour which was an excellent way to learn about the theater's storied past. The guide shared interesting anecdotes about the famous performances and the many renowned composers who have graced its stage.

If you can, attending a performance here is a magical experience. The acoustics of La Fenice are exceptional, and the performances I saw were enhanced by the stunning surroundings. From operas to ballets, the range of shows offered is impressive, and there is something for everyone. If you prefer to enjoy the theater without attending a performance, the guided tours offer a comprehensive look at the building's history and its role in Venice's cultural life.

For those planning to visit, it's a good idea to check the theater's schedule in advance, as performances and tour times can vary. Additionally, booking tickets or tour slots ahead of time can ensure you secure a spot, especially during peak tourist seasons.

Overall, Teatro La Fenice offers an unforgettable experience, whether you're an opera aficionado or simply interested in Venice's rich cultural heritage. The combination of historical charm, architectural beauty, and high-quality performances makes it a must-visit destination in Venice.

Murano Glass Factories

Visiting the Murano Glass Factories is an enchanting experience that offers a glimpse into one of Venice's most famous crafts. Located on Murano Island, these factories are known for their exquisite glassware, which has been crafted here for centuries. To get there, I took the Vaporetto from Venice's main island to Murano. The journey across the lagoon was scenic and added to the anticipation of seeing the famed glasswork up close.

One of the key addresses to visit is the Vetreria Murano Arte, located at Calle dei Vetrai, 9, 30141 Murano. This factory is renowned for its traditional techniques and stunning glass creations. Another notable place is the Murano Glass Museum, situated at Fondamenta Giustinian, 1, 30141 Murano. This museum not only showcases beautiful glass pieces but also provides a comprehensive history of the craft.

Entering the glass factories is generally free if you are just visiting the showrooms and shops. However, some of the factories offer guided tours of their production areas, which usually require a small fee. These tours are highly recommended as they allow you to watch skilled artisans at work, shaping molten glass into intricate designs with remarkable precision. As I joined one of these tours, I was mesmerized by the craftsmanship involved. The artisans' expertise was evident in every piece they created, from delicate vases to elaborate chandeliers.

At the Vetreria Murano Arte, I watched a demonstration where a master glassblower transformed a lump of glowing glass into a beautiful glass vase. The process was fascinating to witness, and the guide provided detailed explanations of the techniques used. After the demonstration, I had the chance to browse their showroom, where I found a range of high-quality glassware, including both traditional and contemporary designs.

The Murano Glass Museum was another highlight. The museum's collection spans from ancient to modern glass art, and the exhibits are beautifully curated. I particularly enjoyed seeing the historical pieces that reflect the evolution of glassmaking on the island. The museum's informative displays also provided context about the glassmaking process and the island's role in its development.

For a more personal experience, I found that visiting smaller, family-run glass factories could be rewarding. These places often offer a more intimate look at the craft and are usually less crowded. The artisans are often happy to explain their work and share their passion for glassmaking.

Shopping for Murano glass can be a bit overwhelming due to the sheer variety of items available. Prices can vary widely, so it's worth taking the time to compare different stores and understand what makes each piece unique. Whether you're looking for a special souvenir or a statement piece for your home, the craftsmanship and beauty of Murano glass make it a worthwhile purchase.

To make the most of your visit, plan to spend a few hours on the island. Allow time to explore the various factories and shops, and don't miss the opportunity to enjoy a leisurely stroll through Murano's charming streets. The island itself is picturesque, with its canals and historic buildings adding to the overall experience.

A visit to the Murano Glass Factories offers a unique and enriching experience, showcasing the artistry and tradition of Venetian glassmaking. The combination of fascinating demonstrations, historical insights, and beautiful glassware makes it a memorable part of any trip to Venice.

The Colorful Island of Burano
Burano, a vibrant island in the Venetian lagoon, is a gem that's well worth a visit. Its charming streets are lined with houses painted in bright, cheerful colors, creating a picturesque setting that's a delight to explore. To reach Burano, I hopped on a Vaporetto from Venice's main island, which was a quick and scenic ride. The journey took about 40 minutes, and as we approached Burano, the colorful facades came into view, promising a delightful experience.

Upon arriving at Burano, I stepped off the Vaporetto at the main stop, which is conveniently located in the heart of the island. The address for the Vaporetto stop is Fondamenta delle Capuccine, 30142 Venezia VE, Italy. From there, it's easy to navigate the island on foot. The vibrant houses and narrow streets create a charming atmosphere, and getting lost in its labyrinthine lanes is part of the fun.

One of the most fascinating aspects of Burano is its lace-making tradition. To learn more about this craft, I visited the Museo del Merletto, located at Piazza Baldassare Galuppi, 187, 30142 Burano VE, Italy. This museum offers free entry and provides an insightful look into the history of lace-making on the island. The exhibits include beautifully intricate lace pieces, and the museum often features demonstrations of the lace-making process. Seeing the delicate artistry up close was truly impressive.

As I wandered through Burano, I was struck by the island's whimsical charm. The houses are painted in a variety of bright colors, each more vivid than the last. This tradition of colorful facades began centuries ago, and it adds to the island's unique character. It's a perfect place for photography, as the vibrant backdrops create stunning visuals.

Dining in Burano is another highlight. I stopped by one of the local trattorias, Trattoria al Gatto Nero, located at Via Giudecca, 88, 30142 Burano VE, Italy. The restaurant offers delicious seafood dishes and has a cozy, welcoming atmosphere. Dining here, I enjoyed fresh local seafood while taking in the lovely views of the canals and colorful houses.

Burano is also known for its lace shops, where you can purchase handcrafted lace items. As I explored the local shops, I found a range of beautiful lace products, from delicate tablecloths to intricate accessories. The shopkeepers are often happy to explain the history and techniques behind their creations, adding to the overall experience.

For a more relaxed experience, I recommend strolling along the canals and enjoying the peaceful ambiance. The island is less crowded than Venice, making it a pleasant place to unwind. I found a quiet spot by the canal, where I sat and took in the serene surroundings, reflecting on the day's discoveries.

A visit to Burano is a delightful escape from the hustle and bustle of Venice. Its colorful houses, rich lace-making tradition, and charming atmosphere make it a memorable destination. Whether you're interested in the local crafts, enjoying a leisurely meal, or simply soaking in the picturesque scenery, Burano offers a unique and enjoyable experience.

Torcello: Venice's Ancient Island

Torcello is a serene and historic island that offers a glimpse into Venice's past, away from the bustle of the more crowded areas. To reach Torcello, I took a Vaporetto from the Fondamenta Nuove stop in Venice. The trip was about 40 minutes, and the peaceful ride provided a great start to the visit. The Vaporetto stop on Torcello is located at Piazza Torcello, 30142 Venezia VE, Italy.

Upon arrival, the island presents a calm and almost timeless atmosphere. There's no need for an entrance fee to explore the island itself, which is a refreshing change from the more tourist-heavy parts of Venice. However, some specific attractions, like the cathedral, do have a small fee for entry.

One of the must-visit spots on Torcello is the Basilica di Santa Maria Assunta, located at Piazza Torcello, 30142 Venezia VE, Italy. The entrance fee here is modest, and it's well worth it for the chance to see the stunning mosaics inside. The basilica, dating back to the 7th century, is known for its remarkable Byzantine mosaics that cover the apse and depict scenes from the Last Judgment. Walking through the basilica, I was struck by the grandeur and historical significance of these ancient artworks. The tranquil ambiance of the church adds to the experience, making it a perfect spot for reflection.

Nearby, I visited the Museo Provinciale di Torcello, located at Piazza Torcello, 30142 Venezia VE, Italy. This small museum offers insights into the island's history and archaeological finds. The museum's exhibits include ancient artifacts and provide context about the island's role in Venice's early history. The entrance is included with the Basilica ticket, which made it convenient to visit both attractions in one go.

Torcello also boasts beautiful natural scenery. I spent some time walking around the island, exploring its lush gardens and peaceful canals. The island's natural beauty contrasts sharply with the bustling city of Venice, offering a more relaxed and contemplative experience. One highlight is the Devil's Bridge (Ponte del Diavolo), a charming and mysterious stone bridge that adds to the island's allure.

For a leisurely meal, I enjoyed dining at Trattoria Alla Madonna, located at Via Torcello, 30142 Venezia VE, Italy. This quaint restaurant offers traditional Venetian cuisine and a pleasant outdoor seating area. Dining here allowed me to savor local dishes while enjoying the serene surroundings of Torcello.

Exploring Torcello, I found that it's a great place to unwind and soak in the history and natural beauty of Venice. The island's quiet streets and historic sites offer a welcome contrast to the more crowded areas of Venice, making it an ideal destination for those seeking a more peaceful and reflective experience. Whether you're interested in history, art, or simply enjoying a tranquil setting, Torcello provides a unique and enriching visit.

CHAPTER 7.
HIDDEN GEMS AND OFF-THE-BEATEN-PATH EXPERIENCE

Exploring the Secret Gardens of Venice

Venice is renowned for its stunning canals and historic buildings, but one of its lesser-known treasures is its secret gardens. These hidden green spaces offer a serene escape from the bustling city and are perfect for a quiet stroll or a moment of reflection.

One of the most enchanting gardens I discovered is the Giardino della Fondazione Querini Stampalia. Located at Campo Santa Maria Formosa, 5252 Venezia VE, Italy, this garden is part of the Querini Stampalia Foundation, which is housed in a beautiful historic building. To get there, I took a Vaporetto to the Fondamenta Nuove stop and then walked about ten minutes. The garden is an oasis of calm, with lush greenery and a beautifully designed layout that contrasts with the busy streets of Venice. It's a wonderful spot to relax, read a book, or simply enjoy the peaceful atmosphere. The entrance to the garden is free, and it's open during the foundation's regular hours.

Another hidden gem is the Giardino delle Rose, located at Calle delle Rose, 30122 Venezia VE, Italy. This small, charming garden is tucked away in the heart of Venice and can be reached by taking a Vaporetto to the Rialto stop and then walking for about fifteen minutes. The garden features a variety of roses and other flowering plants, providing a lovely spot for a leisurely walk or to sit and enjoy the flowers. It's a quieter place compared to the more famous gardens, making it a perfect retreat for those seeking solitude.

For a more extensive garden experience, the Royal Gardens of Venice (Giardini Reali) are also worth a visit. Situated near St. Mark's Square, the entrance is at Piazzetta dei Leoncini, 30124 Venezia VE, Italy. To get there, I walked from St. Mark's Basilica, which is just a short distance away. These gardens are part of the complex around the historic Doge's Palace and offer expansive green spaces with beautifully manicured lawns and a variety of plant species. The gardens are a great place to relax and take in the beauty of Venice from a different perspective. There is a small entrance fee, but the lush surroundings and the opportunity to unwind make it worthwhile.

One of my favorite secret gardens was the Garden of Palazzo Venier dei Leoni. Located at Dorsoduro 701, 30123 Venezia VE, Italy, this garden is part of the Peggy Guggenheim Collection. To reach it, I took a Vaporetto to the Accademia stop and walked a short distance. The garden is a tranquil retreat featuring a mix of sculptures and manicured greenery. While the Peggy Guggenheim Collection itself has an entrance fee, the garden offers a peaceful respite and an opportunity to enjoy some art and nature combined.

Exploring these secret gardens in Venice, I found that they provide a refreshing break from the city's famous landmarks and busy streets. They offer a chance to experience Venice's beauty from a different angle, away from the crowds. Whether you're a garden enthusiast or simply looking for a quiet place to relax, these hidden gems are worth seeking out during your visit.

Visiting the Libreria Acqua Alta

Visiting the Libreria Acqua Alta in Venice is like stepping into a charming, literary dream. This quirky bookstore, located at Calle Lunga Santa Maria Formosa, 5176, 30122 Venezia VE, Italy, is renowned for its unique ambiance and eclectic collection of books.

To get to Libreria Acqua Alta, I took a Vaporetto to the Rialto stop and then enjoyed a pleasant walk through the winding streets of Venice. It's about a fifteen-minute walk from the Rialto Bridge, which allowed me to soak in the city's picturesque alleyways and canals along the way.

As soon as I entered the bookstore, I was greeted by an array of books stored in the most unconventional ways. The store's name, "Acqua Alta," which means "high water," reflects its creative solution to Venice's frequent flooding. Books are stacked in bathtubs, old gondolas, and even a rowboat, which adds a whimsical touch to the experience. The shop's owner, who is known for his friendly demeanor, has created this charming chaos as a way to protect the books from the frequent acqua alta, or high water, that affects the city.

One of the most delightful features of Libreria Acqua Alta is the outdoor area, where you can find more books and some lovely seating that overlooks a canal. Here, you can relax and enjoy a peaceful moment while flipping through a book or just taking in the beautiful view.

In addition to its fascinating book displays, the store has a wonderful collection of vintage books, maps, and prints. Each corner of the shop seems to hold a new surprise, and I found myself discovering hidden gems among the piles of books. Whether you're looking for a rare find or just enjoy browsing through old literature, Libreria Acqua Alta is a treasure trove.

For those interested in photography, this bookstore offers fantastic photo opportunities. The colorful, chaotic arrangements of books and the distinctive setting make for great snapshots, capturing the essence of Venice's unique charm.

I also appreciated how the store's staff were eager to share stories about their collection and the shop's history. They were genuinely passionate about books and Venice, making the visit even more enjoyable.

Visiting Libreria Acqua Alta is a must for anyone who loves books or enjoys experiencing places with a bit of quirky character. It offers a unique glimpse into the literary culture of Venice and a chance to explore a bookstore that has turned its challenges into a delightful experience.

Scuola Grande di San Rocco

The Scuola Grande di San Rocco is one of Venice's hidden gems, a place where art and history blend beautifully. Located at Campo San Rocco, 3052, 30125 Venezia VE, Italy, it's nestled in the San Polo district. This stunning building, built in the late 16th century, is renowned for its remarkable collection of artworks by the Venetian master Tintoretto.

To reach the Scuola Grande di San Rocco, I started from the Rialto Bridge, taking a leisurely stroll through the winding streets of Venice. It's about a 10-minute walk, and the route is lined with charming shops and cafes, making the journey itself quite enjoyable.

As I approached the Scuola, its grand façade immediately caught my eye. The building's intricate architecture hints at the marvels inside. Stepping through the doors, I was greeted by a serene and awe-inspiring atmosphere. The main attraction here is the incredible collection of Tintoretto's paintings that adorn the walls and ceilings. Each room is a masterpiece in itself, showcasing scenes from the life of Christ and the Virgin Mary, all executed with Tintoretto's characteristic dramatic flair and vivid color.

One of the highlights was the Sala dell'Albergo, the room where the members of the Scuola used to meet. The walls and ceiling are covered with Tintoretto's paintings, and the sheer scale and detail of these works are breathtaking. It felt like being enveloped in a living gallery, where each painting seemed to tell a story of its own.

I also visited the Sala dell'Anatomia, which holds a collection of anatomical drawings by the famous Venetian artist. These were fascinating to see, especially considering their historical context and the skill with which Tintoretto executed them.

The atmosphere inside is peaceful, allowing you to take your time and truly appreciate the artistry. I spent several hours here, moving slowly from room to room, soaking in the intricate details and vibrant colors.

For those interested in history and art, the Scuola Grande di San Rocco offers a profound experience. The building itself is a piece of history, and the artworks within are among the finest examples of Venetian Renaissance art. It's also worth noting that there's a modest entrance fee, but it's well worth it for the quality and depth of the experience.

When visiting, I recommend taking a guided tour if available. The guides provide valuable insights into the artwork and the history of the Scuola, enhancing the overall visit. Also, be sure to check the opening hours before you go, as they can vary.

In summary, the Scuola Grande di San Rocco is a must-visit for art enthusiasts and anyone interested in Venice's rich cultural heritage. Its impressive collection of Tintoretto's masterpieces, coupled with its historical significance, makes it a memorable stop on any Venetian itinerary.

The Quiet Charm of Giudecca

Giudecca is a tranquil island in Venice that offers a serene escape from the bustling heart of the city. Located just across the canal from the main islands, Giudecca is known for its peaceful ambiance and charming, less crowded streets.

To reach Giudecca, I took a Vaporetto from the main island, a water bus that operates regularly and is an easy way to get there. The Vaporetto docks at several stops on Giudecca, including the main stop at Giudecca 2, making it convenient to explore.

Upon arrival, the first thing that struck me was the contrast to the lively areas of Venice. Giudecca has a relaxed vibe with wide, open spaces and stunning views of the city. The waterfront promenade offers lovely views of the Venetian skyline and is a great place for a leisurely stroll.

One of the highlights of my visit was the Church of the Redeemer, or Chiesa del Santissimo Redentore, located at the western end of the island. This historic church is known for its beautiful architecture and the annual Festa del Redentore, a major festival celebrated with fireworks and boat parties. Even if you're not visiting during the festival, the church's serene interior and impressive design are worth seeing. The address is Sestiere Giudecca, 601, 30133 Venezia VE, Italy.

Another gem on Giudecca is the Molino Stucky Hilton, a historic hotel with a fascinating past. While not a traditional tourist attraction, the hotel itself is an architectural marvel and offers great views from its rooftop bar. It's also a nice spot for a drink or a meal if you want to soak in the atmosphere without venturing into the busier parts of Venice.

If you're interested in art, a visit to the Fondazione Giorgio Cini is a must. Located at Isola di San Giorgio Maggiore, 30133 Venezia VE, Italy, just a short Vaporetto ride away from Giudecca, this cultural foundation hosts a range of exhibitions and events in a beautiful setting. The library and the restored historic buildings on the island make for an enriching visit.

For a taste of local life, I explored the small shops and cafes scattered around Giudecca. The island has a few hidden gems where you can enjoy a coffee or a meal while taking in the peaceful surroundings. The local eateries offer a more authentic Venetian experience away from the typical tourist spots.

In terms of budget-friendly options, Giudecca has a variety of small, family-run restaurants where you can enjoy delicious Venetian cuisine without the hefty price tags found in more touristy areas. Wandering around the island, I discovered charming places with reasonable prices, perfect for travelers on a budget.

Giudecca offers a quiet charm that's a delightful contrast to the bustling center of Venice. Its serene atmosphere, stunning views, and hidden treasures make it a wonderful place to relax and experience a different side of the city. Whether you're looking to escape the crowds or simply enjoy a peaceful day, Giudecca is well worth a visit.

Discovering the Jewish Ghetto

Discovering the Jewish Ghetto in Venice is like stepping into a rich historical narrative that's deeply intertwined with the city's past. Located in the Cannaregio district, this area is one of the oldest Jewish ghettos in the world. I found it to be an enlightening and poignant part of my visit to Venice.

To get to the Jewish Ghetto, I hopped on a Vaporetto, the public water bus, and got off at the "Ghetto" stop. The Vaporetto is an easy way to travel around Venice and offers a convenient and scenic route to the ghetto. From the stop, it's a short walk to the heart of the area.

The Jewish Ghetto is a maze of narrow streets and charming squares that seem to tell stories of the past. The area is home to several synagogues, each with its unique history. The oldest of these is the Scuola Grande Tedesca, located at Campo del Ghetto Nuovo, 30121 Venezia VE, Italy. The synagogues are spread across different buildings, reflecting the diverse nature of the Jewish community that lived here.

One of the highlights of my visit was the Jewish Museum of Venice, situated at Campo del Ghetto Nuovo, 30121 Venezia VE, Italy. The museum is a treasure trove of artifacts, documents, and displays that offer a deep dive into the history and culture of Venice's Jewish community. I enjoyed exploring the exhibits, which include everything from historical documents to traditional clothing. The museum also offers guided tours that provide additional insights into the ghetto's history.

Walking through the ghetto, I came across several beautiful synagogues, such as the Great Synagogue, which is located at Campo del Ghetto Nuovo, 30121 Venezia VE, Italy. It's an impressive building with stunning architecture. While the synagogues are not always open to the public, I found that many offer tours or have specific visiting hours, so it's a good idea to check in advance.

The area is also known for its kosher restaurants and bakeries, which offer a taste of traditional Jewish cuisine. I stopped by a small bakery, where I tried some delicious traditional pastries. The local eateries in the ghetto are a great way to experience authentic Jewish dishes and enjoy a meal in a historically significant setting.

For those interested in shopping, there are small shops in the ghetto that sell Jewish-themed souvenirs and books. I found a few charming stores where I could pick up unique gifts and mementos related to Jewish culture and history.

The Jewish Ghetto is a must-visit for anyone interested in history and culture. It provides a glimpse into Venice's rich and diverse past, offering a peaceful and reflective experience. The area's narrow streets, historic synagogues, and cultural landmarks make it a fascinating place to explore and learn about the contributions and experiences of the Jewish community in Venice.

Venetian Mask Workshops

Venetian mask workshops offer a unique and immersive way to experience Venice's rich tradition of mask-making. These workshops let you dive into a centuries-old craft that's closely tied to the city's famous Carnival.

One of the most memorable mask workshops I attended was at Ca' Macana, located at Dorsoduro 3163, 30123 Venezia VE, Italy. Getting there was straightforward. I took a Vaporetto to the "Accademia" stop and then enjoyed a pleasant walk through the charming streets of Dorsoduro. The workshop is tucked away in a picturesque corner of Venice, making the journey part of the adventure.

Ca' Macana is renowned for its authentic approach to Venetian mask-making. When I arrived, I was greeted by the friendly staff who guided me through the history of mask-making and the different styles used during the Venetian Carnival. The workshop itself is a creative haven filled with colorful masks, paints, and materials.

During the workshop, I had the chance to design and create my own mask. The process began with selecting a basic mask shape, and then we got to work decorating it using paints, feathers, and other embellishments. The instructors were incredibly knowledgeable and offered plenty of tips and techniques to help bring our designs to life. I found it fascinating to learn about the different mask types, such as the traditional Bauta and Colombina masks, and how they are used in Venice's Carnival celebrations.

Another great place for a mask-making experience is Atelier Pietro Longhi, located at San Marco 4871, 30124 Venezia VE, Italy. I visited this atelier as well and was equally impressed. The workshop here also starts with a brief introduction to the history and significance of Venetian masks. The atmosphere was both welcoming and inspiring. I was able to choose from a variety of mask designs and then spent a few hours crafting and decorating. The hands-on experience was both educational and enjoyable.

Both of these workshops offer a wonderful way to delve into Venetian culture. They provide not only a creative outlet but also an educational experience about a cherished local tradition. The finished masks make for unique souvenirs that capture the essence of Venice's Carnival spirit.

For those who are budget-conscious, it's worth noting that mask workshops vary in price. Some workshops offer group sessions or smaller, more affordable classes, which can be a great way to experience the craft without breaking the bank. Additionally, checking for any special offers or discounts can help make the experience more affordable.

Participating in a Venetian mask workshop is a delightful way to connect with Venice's artistic heritage. Whether you're a seasoned artist or just looking for a fun and creative activity, these workshops offer a memorable and hands-on way to engage with the city's vibrant culture.

CHAPTER 8.
CULTURAL EXPERIENCES

The Venice Carnival: A World of Masks and Mystery

The Venice Carnival is a magical time when the city transforms into a colorful stage of masks, costumes, and festivities. Held annually in February, this grand celebration has been a part of Venetian culture for centuries, and experiencing it firsthand is like stepping into a living work of art.

One of the best ways to dive into the Venice Carnival is by visiting the main areas where festivities take place. The heart of the celebration is in Piazza San Marco, which is where I found myself on my visit. This grand square, located at Piazza San Marco, 30124 Venezia VE, Italy, becomes a vibrant hub of activity during the carnival. To get there, you can take a Vaporetto to the "San Marco" stop or enjoy a leisurely walk through the charming streets of Venice.

As you enter Piazza San Marco, you'll be greeted by a sea of elegantly dressed figures in elaborate masks and costumes. The atmosphere is electric with street performers, live music, and a constant buzz of excitement. The iconic masks and costumes, which range from intricate lace and feathered creations to bold and colorful designs, truly bring the carnival to life. It's worth taking some time to simply wander around and admire the artistry on display.

One of the highlights of the Venice Carnival is the "Masquerade Ball," which is held in various historic venues across the city. I had the chance to attend a ball at the Ca' Vendramin Calergi, located at Campo S. Stae, 2070, 30135 Venezia VE, Italy. This stunning palace provided a breathtaking backdrop for the event. To get there, I took a Vaporetto to the "S. Stae" stop and then enjoyed a short walk to the venue. The ball itself was an enchanting experience, with guests dressed in period costumes, dancing to classical music, and enjoying the opulent surroundings.

If you're interested in more traditional carnival activities, don't miss the "Flight of the Angel," which takes place in Piazza San Marco. This spectacular event involves a costumed figure, known as the "Angel," descending from the Campanile (bell tower) on a zip line into the square. The event marks the official opening of the carnival and is a thrilling spectacle that draws crowds from all over.

For a deeper dive into the carnival's history and traditions, consider visiting the Museo della Maschera, located at Calle del Campanile, 30124 Venezia VE, Italy. This museum offers fascinating insights into the art of mask-making and the history of the Venice Carnival. It's a short walk from Piazza San Marco, and exploring the museum provides a wonderful context for the elaborate costumes and masks you see throughout the city.

The Venice Carnival is not just about grand events; it's also about enjoying the city's charm in a festive atmosphere. Strolling along the canals and through the narrow streets, you'll encounter street performers, food stalls, and small-scale celebrations that add to the carnival's charm.

For budget travelers, there are plenty of ways to enjoy the carnival without spending a fortune. Many of the street performances and public festivities are free to attend. Additionally, consider visiting local bakeries and cafes to sample traditional carnival treats like "frittelle" (sweet fried dough) and "baicoli" (crisp biscuits), which are delicious and budget-friendly.

The Venice Carnival is a captivating experience that offers a glimpse into a world of masks, mystery, and tradition. Whether you're attending grand balls, watching the Flight of the Angel, or simply enjoying the festive atmosphere in the streets, the carnival provides an unforgettable opportunity to immerse yourself in Venetian culture.

Art and Architecture: From Byzantine to Baroque

Venice is a city where art and architecture weave a rich tapestry, reflecting centuries of history from Byzantine mosaics to Baroque opulence. Exploring this artistic evolution can be a captivating journey.

To start your adventure in Venetian art and architecture, head to the Basilica di San Marco, located at Piazza San Marco, 30124 Venezia VE, Italy. This iconic church is a stunning example of Byzantine art, characterized by its grand domes and intricate mosaics. I remember my visit vividly; stepping inside felt like entering a golden realm, with every inch of the walls and ceiling covered in shimmering mosaics. To get there, you can easily take a Vaporetto to the "San Marco" stop or enjoy a scenic walk through Venice's narrow streets.

Next, make your way to the Doge's Palace, also located at Piazza San Marco, 30124 Venezia VE, Italy. This Gothic masterpiece was once the residence of the Venetian Doge and is a perfect example of Venetian Gothic architecture. The palace's façade, with its intricate marble patterns and ornate details, is truly breathtaking. Inside, you'll find a treasure trove of art and history, including the famous Bridge of Sighs. Getting there is straightforward from the Basilica di San Marco; just follow the signs or enjoy the short walk.

For a taste of Renaissance architecture, visit the Scuola Grande di San Rocco, situated at San Polo, 3052, 30125 Venezia VE, Italy. This building, built in the late 16th century, is renowned for its stunning frescoes by Tintoretto. The frescoes are so immersive that they feel almost like stepping into a living painting. To get there, take a Vaporetto to the "S. Stae" stop and walk a bit to reach this artistic gem.

To explore Baroque art and architecture, head to the Church of Santa Maria della Salute, located at Dorsoduro, 1, 30123 Venezia VE, Italy. This church, with its striking dome and elaborate interior, offers a splendid example of Baroque design. The church's interior is adorned with dramatic and richly detailed decorations, creating a sense of grandeur and emotion. You can reach Santa Maria della Salute by taking a Vaporetto to the "Salute" stop.

For a broader view of Venetian art across different periods, visit the Gallerie dell'Accademia, located at Campo della Carità, 1050, 30123 Venezia VE, Italy. This museum houses an extensive collection of Venetian art, from Byzantine icons to Renaissance masterpieces. Walking through the gallery, you'll encounter works by famous artists like Titian and Bellini. To get there, take a Vaporetto to the "Accademia" stop or enjoy a leisurely walk from nearby attractions.

Exploring Venice's art and architecture is like stepping through a time machine. Each building and artwork tells a story, from the glittering mosaics of Byzantine times to the opulent details of the Baroque era. Whether you're admiring the intricate designs of the Basilica di San Marco or the dramatic frescoes of the Scuola Grande di San Rocco, Venice offers a rich tapestry of artistic and architectural marvels.

Music and Opera in Venice

Venice is a city with a deep and passionate connection to music and opera, offering experiences that resonate with its rich cultural history.

If you're keen on experiencing Venetian music, start with a visit to Teatro La Fenice. This historic opera house, located at Campo San Fantin, 1965, 30124 Venezia VE, Italy, is a cornerstone of Venice's musical heritage. It has hosted some of the greatest operas and is renowned for its stunning interior and acoustics. Getting there is easy; you can take a Vaporetto to the "San Marco" stop and enjoy a pleasant walk through the heart of Venice.

When you step inside La Fenice, you're greeted by opulent décor with golden chandeliers and plush seating that instantly sets the mood for a grand performance. I vividly recall attending an opera there; the atmosphere was electric, and the acoustics made every note feel alive. To make the most of your visit, check their schedule in advance and consider booking tickets for a performance.

Another iconic venue is the Basilica di San Marco, located at Piazza San Marco, 30124 Venezia VE, Italy. Known for its awe-inspiring mosaics and architectural beauty, the Basilica also hosts occasional classical music concerts. The experience of hearing live music in such a historic and sacred space is unforgettable. To get there, simply follow the signs from major landmarks or take a Vaporetto to the "San Marco" stop.

For a more intimate musical experience, visit the Vivaldi Church, or Chiesa di Santa Maria della Pietà, at Castello, 3701, 30122 Venezia VE, Italy. This church is famously associated with Antonio Vivaldi, one of Venice's most celebrated composers. The church occasionally hosts concerts featuring Vivaldi's music. Attending a performance here is like stepping back in time to the Baroque era. It's a short Vaporetto ride from central Venice, followed by a brief walk.

Venice also offers a rich array of outdoor musical experiences. Wander through the Piazza San Marco in the evening, where you might catch live music from the cafés and orchestras. The lively atmosphere, combined with the stunning backdrop of the square, creates a magical experience. Many of the historic cafés around the square feature live classical music performances, providing a delightful soundtrack to your evening.

To fully immerse yourself in Venice's musical heritage, consider a guided tour that focuses on the city's musical history. These tours often include visits to historic sites related to famous composers and performances, providing deeper insight into Venice's vibrant music scene.

Whether you're attending a grand opera at La Fenice, enjoying a classical concert at the Vivaldi Church, or simply soaking in the atmosphere of Piazza San Marco, Venice offers a musical journey that's rich in history and enchantment.

Venice's Festivals and Events

Festa della Sensa

I'd always wanted to experience a traditional Venetian festival, so when I heard about the Festa della Sensa, I knew I had to be there. The idea of a religious celebration with a maritime theme sounded like a fascinating mix of history, culture, and pageantry.

As the day of the festival approached, I found myself getting increasingly excited. I'd read about the elaborate preparations that went into the event, including the construction of a floating platform known as the "machina" that would be used for the blessing of the sea.

On the day of the Festa, I arrived at St. Mark's Square early to secure a good spot. The square was already buzzing with activity, as people dressed in traditional Venetian garb mingled and prepared for the festivities.

I struck up a conversation with a friendly-looking woman named Maria, who was wearing a beautiful lace gown. She told me that she had been attending the Festa della Sensa for as long as she could remember.

"It's a tradition that goes back centuries," she explained. "The festival is a way to celebrate Venice's maritime heritage and to give thanks for the sea's bounty."

As Maria and I chatted, we watched the procession of gondolas and other historic boats make their way towards the Grand Canal. The boats were adorned with colorful flags and banners, and the air was filled with the sound of music and cheering.

Finally, the machina was towed into position, and the religious ceremony began. A priest blessed the sea, and the crowd erupted in applause. As the fireworks lit up the night sky, I couldn't help but feel a sense of awe and wonder.

The Festa della Sensa was everything I had hoped for and more. It was a truly unforgettable experience that allowed me to connect with Venice's rich history and culture. And as I made my way back to my hotel that night, I knew I would never forget the memory of the floating platform, the colorful boats, and the friendly people I had met along the way.

Venice's Nightlife: Bars, Clubs, and Jazz Venues

Venice's nightlife is a charming mix of sophisticated venues and lively spots that cater to various tastes, from relaxed bars to high-energy nightclubs.

For a taste of Venice's bar scene, start with the classic Harry's Bar, located at Calle Vallaresso 1323, 30124 Venezia VE, Italy. This iconic bar is renowned for its Bellini cocktails and has a storied history that includes serving famous patrons like Ernest Hemingway. The atmosphere here is elegant yet relaxed, perfect for sipping a cocktail while soaking in the refined ambiance. Another great spot is Al Timon, situated on Fondamenta della Misericordia 2615, 30121 Venezia VE, Italy. This bar offers a more laid-back vibe with a fantastic selection of craft beers and local wines. The outdoor seating by the canal provides a scenic backdrop that's ideal for a casual evening.

When it comes to live music, Venice has several noteworthy venues. The Jazz Club "Cafè Florièn," found at Piazza San Marco, 30124 Venezia VE, Italy, offers an intimate setting with performances featuring jazz and classical music. The schedule often includes local talents and occasional visiting artists, creating a rich, musical experience in a historic café setting. For something a bit more modern, head to "Teatro Toniolo" in Mestre, at Via Giorgione 5, 30174 Mestre VE, Italy. This venue features a range of genres from rock to electronic, with performances typically scheduled throughout the week. The energy here is vibrant, making it a great place to enjoy live music in a dynamic environment.

If you're looking to dance the night away, Venice offers a selection of nightclubs that cater to different tastes. "Piccolo Mondo," located at Via Santa Maria della Pietà, 30122 Venezia VE, Italy, is a popular choice for those who enjoy high-energy dance music. This nightclub features resident DJs and special events, creating a lively atmosphere for a night out. Another hotspot is "Vega Club," found at Viale Ancona 1, 30172 Mestre VE, Italy. Known for its sophisticated vibe and varied music styles, Vega Club frequently hosts guest DJs and themed parties, making it a vibrant destination for nightlife enthusiasts.

Venice's nightlife is deeply intertwined with local culture. Locals often enjoy leisurely dinners that can extend into late-night socializing. It's customary to have a glass of wine or an aperitivo like a spritz in the early evening, which transitions into dinner and then possibly into nightlife activities. The concept of "aperitivo" is central to Venetian culture, so be sure to enjoy this ritual as part of your experience.

For a unique experience, seek out hidden gems like "Osteria Ai Promessi Sposi," located at Campo San Giacomo dell'Orio 1476, 30135 Venezia VE, Italy. This charming eatery offers a cozy atmosphere with delicious, homemade Venetian dishes. Another secret spot is "Bar al Timon," a small, tucked-away bar on Fondamenta della Misericordia, known for its relaxed vibe and excellent local wines.

In terms of safety and practicality, Venice is generally safe at night, but like any city, it's wise to stay aware of your surroundings. Public transportation like Vaporetto runs late into the night, but always checks the schedules to avoid any inconvenience. It's also a good idea to stick to well-lit areas and avoid isolated spots, especially if you're unfamiliar with the city.

Venice's nightlife scene offers a rich tapestry of experiences, from elegant bars and intimate live music venues to lively nightclubs and hidden gems. Embrace the local customs, explore different areas, and enjoy the vibrant atmosphere that makes Venice a captivating destination after dark.

Venice's Artisan Crafts: Lace, Glass, and Masks

Venice is famous for its rich tradition of artisan crafts, with lace, glass, and masks being three of the most celebrated. Each craft has a long history and contributes to the city's unique charm.

The art of lace-making in Venice is most closely associated with the island of Burano. Here, you can visit the shops and workshops that specialize in this delicate craft. The lace made on Burano is known for its intricate patterns and fine quality. One of the best places to explore this tradition is the "Museo del Merletto" (Lace Museum) located at Piazza Baldassarre Galuppi 187, 30142 Burano VE, Italy. The museum showcases the history of lace-making and exhibits beautiful examples of Burano lace. You can also find local artisans creating lace pieces right in their shops, where you can purchase handmade lace items or even watch the craftsmen at work.

Murano, another famous Venetian island, is renowned for its glass-making. The glass factories here have been producing exquisite glassware for centuries. To experience this craft, visit one of the many glass workshops on the island. One notable place is the "Vetreria Murano Arte," located at Fondamenta Giustinian 12, 30141 Murano VE, Italy. Here, you can watch live demonstrations of glassblowing and see artisans create stunning glass pieces. The craftsmanship is impressive, and you can buy beautiful glass objects ranging from elegant vases to intricate sculptures. It's also worth exploring the "Museo del Vetro" (Glass Museum) at Palazzo Giustinian, Fondamenta

Giustinian 8, 30141 Murano VE, Italy, which offers a comprehensive look at the history and techniques of Murano glass.

Venetian masks are another iconic craft that you'll encounter throughout the city. These masks are a traditional part of Venice's Carnival and are known for their elaborate designs. To find these masks, visit the "Ca' del Sol" shop located at Calle delle Botteghe 3472, 30124 Venezia VE, Italy. This shop offers a wide range of beautifully crafted masks, each with unique designs and colors. You can also learn about the history and symbolism behind these masks. For an immersive experience, consider participating in a mask-making workshop, where you can create your own Venetian mask under the guidance of skilled artisans.

Exploring Venice's artisan crafts provides a deeper appreciation for the city's rich cultural heritage. From the delicate lace of Burano to the vibrant glass of Murano and the ornate masks that adorn Carnival, these crafts offer a tangible connection to Venice's history and artistry. Be sure to take the time to visit these islands, watch the artisans at work, and perhaps bring home a piece of Venice's craftsmanship as a lasting memory.

CHAPTER 9.
DAY TRIPS FROM VENICE

Visiting the Prosecco Wine Region

Visiting the Prosecco Wine Region is a delightful experience that combines stunning landscapes with the joy of tasting Italy's famous sparkling wine. Located in the Veneto region, just a short drive from Venice, the Prosecco hills stretch between the towns of Conegliano and Valdobbiadene. This area is renowned for producing Prosecco, a light and refreshing sparkling wine that has become beloved worldwide.

Getting to the Prosecco region from Venice is relatively easy. You can take a train from Venice to Conegliano, which is about an hour's journey. From Conegliano, the best way to explore the region is by car, as it allows you to visit various wineries at your own pace. If you prefer not to drive, there are also guided wine tours available that include transportation, which can be a relaxing way to enjoy the region without worrying about navigating the roads.

As you travel through the rolling hills of the Prosecco region, you'll be treated to breathtaking views of vineyards stretching as far as the eye can see. The landscape is dotted with charming villages, historic churches, and elegant villas, making the journey as enjoyable as the wine itself.

One of the highlights of visiting the Prosecco region is touring the local wineries, known as "cantine." Many of these wineries are family-run, and they warmly welcome visitors to learn about their wine-making process. During a typical visit, you'll get to tour the vineyards, see how the grapes are harvested and processed, and, of course, taste a variety of Prosecco wines. Some of the well-known wineries in the area include "Nino Franco" in Valdobbiadene and "Bisol" in Santo Stefano. Both offer guided tours and tastings, where you can sample different types of Prosecco, from the crisp and dry "Brut" to the slightly sweeter "Extra Dry."

In addition to wine tasting, the region offers plenty of opportunities for dining. Many wineries have their own restaurants or collaborate with local eateries to provide meals that pair perfectly with their wines. Enjoying a meal in the Prosecco hills is a special experience, where you can savor local dishes like risotto with Prosecco or fresh pasta with seasonal ingredients, all while sipping on a glass of the sparkling wine.

If you have more time, consider exploring some of the picturesque towns in the region. Conegliano is known for its historic center and castle, while Valdobbiadene is the heart of the Prosecco production area. Both towns offer a glimpse into the local culture and history, with their narrow streets, ancient buildings, and vibrant markets.

Visiting the Prosecco Wine Region is not just about tasting wine; it's about immersing yourself in a beautiful and serene landscape, learning about the traditions of the area, and enjoying the warm hospitality of the locals. Whether you're a wine enthusiast or simply looking for a peaceful escape from the bustle of Venice, the Prosecco hills offer a perfect day trip or weekend getaway. You'll leave with a deeper appreciation for this sparkling wine and fond memories of the scenic Italian countryside.

A Day in Padua

Spending a day in Padua is like stepping into a treasure trove of history, art, and Italian charm. Located just a short train ride from Venice, Padua is often overshadowed by its more famous neighbor, but it has a rich cultural heritage and a relaxed atmosphere that makes it well worth a visit.

As you arrive in Padua, the first thing you'll notice is the city's blend of medieval architecture and lively, modern energy. Start your day at the Prato della Valle, one of the largest squares in Europe. This expansive oval-shaped piazza is surrounded by a canal and lined with statues of famous historical figures. It's a peaceful place to stroll, take in the scenery, and snap some photos of the beautiful surrounding buildings.

From there, head to the Basilica of Saint Anthony of Padua, known locally as "Il Santo." This magnificent church is not only a pilgrimage site but also an architectural wonder. Inside, you'll find the tomb of Saint Anthony, surrounded by intricate sculptures and stunning frescoes. The atmosphere is serene, and whether you're religious or not, the basilica's beauty and historical significance are undeniable.

Next, make your way to the Scrovegni Chapel, home to one of the most important works of art in Italy: Giotto's fresco cycle. These frescoes, which date back to the early 14th century, depict the life of the Virgin Mary and Christ in vivid detail. The colors and expressions are so vibrant that it's hard to believe they're over 700 years old. Due to its popularity, it's wise to book tickets in advance, as entry is limited to preserve the artwork.

After soaking in the art and spirituality, it's time to enjoy some local cuisine. Padua's markets and trattorias offer a taste of authentic Italian flavors. Consider stopping by Piazza delle Erbe or Piazza della Frutta for a bite. These bustling squares are filled with vendors selling fresh produce, cheeses, and meats. Nearby, you can find cozy cafes where you can enjoy a leisurely lunch. Try a dish of bigoli, a thick, spaghetti-like pasta that's a regional specialty, often served with duck ragù.

In the afternoon, explore the University of Padua, one of the oldest universities in the world. It's where Galileo Galilei once taught, and its historic halls are filled with academic heritage. The university's Anatomical Theatre is particularly fascinating; it's the oldest surviving anatomical theater in the world, where students once gathered to learn about the human body.

As your day winds down, take a leisurely walk along the Riviera dei Ponti Romani, a picturesque street that follows the path of the ancient Roman bridge. The walk offers a tranquil setting, with views of the river and charming old buildings that reflect the light of the setting sun.

Before you leave, consider stopping at a local bar for an Aperol Spritz—a popular Venetian aperitif—to toast to a day well spent. Padua may be small compared to Venice, but its rich history, beautiful art, and welcoming vibe make it a delightful destination for anyone looking to experience the heart of Italian culture in just one day.

Exploring the Villas of the Brenta Canal

Exploring the Villas of the Brenta Canal is like stepping back in time to the opulent days of the Venetian Republic. The Brenta Canal, which stretches from Venice to Padua, is lined with magnificent villas that were once the summer retreats of Venetian nobility. These grand homes, surrounded by lush gardens and adorned with exquisite frescoes, offer a glimpse into the luxurious lifestyle of the past.

To begin your journey, you can start in Venice or Padua, both of which are easily accessible by train. From Venice, a bus or a boat ride along the Brenta Canal will take you directly to the villas. One popular option is to take a boat tour, which allows you to enjoy the scenic beauty of the canal while stopping at several villas along the way. If you prefer to travel by road, buses also run along the canal, with stops near the main villas.

The most famous of these villas is Villa Pisani, located in Stra. Often called the "Queen of the Venetian Villas," Villa Pisani is a masterpiece of Baroque architecture. As you approach, the sheer size of the villa is breathtaking. Inside, you can explore room after room filled with ornate furniture, stunning frescoes, and elaborate decorations. One of the highlights is the ballroom, with its grand chandeliers and beautifully painted ceilings. The villa's gardens are equally impressive, featuring a labyrinth that is both fun and challenging to navigate.

Another villa worth visiting is Villa Widmann in Mira. Smaller and more intimate than Villa Pisani, Villa Widmann has a charm all its own. The villa is surrounded by lovely gardens and offers a more personal look at life in the 18th century. The interior is decorated in a Rococo style, with pastel colors and delicate details that create a light, airy atmosphere. The ballroom here is particularly lovely, with its mirrors and chandeliers reflecting the light in a way that makes the room sparkle.

Further along the canal is Villa Foscari, also known as "La Malcontenta." Designed by the famous architect Andrea Palladio, this villa is a perfect example of Palladian architecture, with its symmetrical design and classical proportions. The villa's name, which means "the unhappy one," is said to come from a legend about a woman who was confined there after displeasing her husband. Despite its somewhat somber history, the villa is a beautiful and peaceful place to visit, with frescoes that depict scenes from mythology and a terrace that offers stunning views of the canal.

As you explore the villas, you'll notice that each one has its own unique character and story. Some are grand and imposing, while others are more modest and intimate. But all of them share a connection to the rich cultural and artistic heritage of the Venetian Republic.

To make the most of your day, it's a good idea to plan your route in advance, as there are many villas to choose from. Whether you decide to visit just one or two, or spend the whole day exploring several, you'll find that each villa offers something special. If you're traveling by boat, you'll also enjoy the scenic views along the canal, with its green banks and charming villages.

As the day draws to a close, consider stopping at a local trattoria for a meal. The region is known for its excellent cuisine, with dishes that reflect the flavors of both the land and the sea. Enjoying a meal of fresh pasta or seafood, accompanied by a glass of local wine, is the perfect way to end your day of exploration.

Exploring the Villas of the Brenta Canal is not just about seeing beautiful buildings; it's about experiencing the history, art, and culture of a bygone era. Whether you're an art lover, a history buff, or simply someone who appreciates beauty, this journey offers a rich and rewarding experience.

The Charming Town of Treviso

The town of Treviso, often overshadowed by its more famous neighbor Venice, is a hidden gem that offers a delightful blend of history, culture, and charm. Located just a short train ride from Venice, Treviso is a place where you can wander through quiet streets, enjoy local cuisine, and soak in the relaxed atmosphere that feels worlds away from the busy canals of Venice.

As you arrive in Treviso, the first thing you'll notice is the peacefulness. The town is surrounded by ancient walls and crossed by picturesque canals, giving it a serene and inviting feel. The historic center is a maze of narrow cobblestone streets, lined with elegant buildings and small squares that seem to appear around every corner.

One of the highlights of Treviso is Piazza dei Signori, the main square in the heart of the town. This bustling square is the perfect place to start your exploration. The square is home to the Palazzo dei Trecento, a historic building that dates back to the 13th century. Nearby, you'll find the Loggia dei Cavalieri, another beautiful example of medieval architecture. As you stroll through the square, take a moment to admire the charming cafés and shops that line the streets, offering everything from local delicacies to handmade crafts.

Another must-see in Treviso is the Cathedral of San Pietro. The cathedral, with its impressive neoclassical façade, houses some remarkable works of art, including frescoes by the famous Venetian painter Titian. The interior of the cathedral is equally stunning, with a serene atmosphere that invites quiet reflection. Just outside the cathedral, you can explore the Romanesque crypt, which adds another layer of history to your visit.

Treviso is also known for its canals, which are less crowded but just as enchanting as those in Venice. A walk along the Canale dei Buranelli is a must. The canal is named after the fishermen from the island of Burano who once lived here, and it's lined with beautiful old buildings and small bridges. The reflections of the houses in the water create a postcard-perfect scene, especially in the early morning or late afternoon when the light is soft.

As you explore the town, you'll also discover its connection to the culinary world. Treviso is the birthplace of tiramisu, the famous Italian dessert. Many local cafés and restaurants claim to have the original recipe, so it's a great opportunity to taste this delicious treat in the town where it was created. Another local specialty is radicchio, a type of bitter red lettuce that is used in many dishes. If you're visiting in the winter months, you'll find it featured prominently on menus throughout the town.

Treviso is also home to several interesting museums, including the Museo Civico di Santa Caterina. Housed in a former convent, the museum features a collection of art and artifacts that tell the story of Treviso's rich history. The museum is small but well-curated, making it an enjoyable stop for those interested in learning more about the town's past.

If you're looking for some outdoor time, the town offers several parks and gardens where you can relax and enjoy the scenery. The Parco degli Alberi Parlanti is a beautiful green space with walking paths, ponds, and plenty of benches where you can sit and enjoy the tranquility. It's a great spot for a leisurely picnic or just to take a break from exploring.

To truly experience the charm of Treviso, take your time. The town is small enough to explore on foot, and there's no need to rush. Whether you're sitting in a café enjoying a cappuccino, wandering through the quiet streets, or simply taking in the views along the canals, Treviso offers a slower pace that is both refreshing and rejuvenating.

Getting to Treviso is easy. From Venice, you can take a direct train from Santa Lucia station. The journey takes about 30 minutes, making Treviso an ideal day trip destination. Once you arrive, the town's compact size means that everything is within walking distance, so you can explore at your own pace.

Treviso is a town that delights with its quiet charm, rich history, and delicious cuisine. It's a place where you can escape the crowds, discover hidden corners, and enjoy the simple pleasures of life in an authentic Italian setting. Whether you're a history buff, a food lover, or just looking for a peaceful retreat, Treviso offers a memorable experience that will leave you wanting to return.

The Natural Beauty of the Po Delta

The Po Delta, located in northern Italy, is a stunning natural area where the Po River meets the Adriatic Sea. It's a vast and peaceful landscape, characterized by wide lagoons, dense wetlands, and a maze of canals that stretch as far as the eye can see. The Po Delta is one of Europe's most important wetlands, making it a paradise for nature lovers, birdwatchers, and anyone looking to escape the hustle and bustle of city life.

Visiting the Po Delta is like stepping into a different world, where the rhythm of life is slower and more connected to nature. As you explore the area, you'll be surrounded by the serene beauty of the wetlands, with their shimmering waters, tall reeds, and the calls of birds echoing in the distance. The landscape is flat, making it perfect for long, leisurely walks or bike rides along the many paths that crisscross the region.

One of the best ways to experience the Po Delta is by boat. Taking a boat tour allows you to glide through the quiet canals, getting up close to the wildlife and enjoying the peaceful atmosphere. You'll likely see a variety of birds, including herons, egrets, and even flamingos, which are a highlight for many visitors. The boat tours often include knowledgeable guides who can share insights about the local ecosystem and the unique characteristics of the Po Delta.

For those who prefer to stay on land, the Po Delta is crisscrossed with walking and cycling paths that take you through some of the most scenic parts of the region. The paths are well-marked and easy to follow, making them accessible for people of all ages and fitness levels. As you walk or cycle, you'll pass through small villages, fields of crops, and wooded areas, all with the constant backdrop of the wetlands. It's a great way to slow down, breathe in the fresh air, and fully appreciate the natural beauty around you.

The Po Delta is also home to several nature reserves, such as the Parco del Delta del Po, where you can explore a variety of habitats, from salt marshes to sand dunes. These reserves are perfect for a day of exploration, offering opportunities to see rare plants and animals that thrive in this unique environment. Many of the reserves have observation towers or hides where you can quietly watch the wildlife without disturbing them.

If you're interested in history, the Po Delta has a rich cultural heritage as well. The area has been shaped by human hands for centuries, with ancient villages, historic canals, and traditional fishing huts known as "casoni" dotting the landscape. Some of these huts have been converted into museums or visitor centers where you can learn about the traditional ways of life in the delta, including fishing and salt production.

Another interesting aspect of the Po Delta is its connection to the sea. The region's proximity to the Adriatic means that you can enjoy both the fresh and saltwater environments. In some areas, you'll find stretches of sandy beaches where you can relax and take in the coastal scenery. The combination of wetland and coastal landscapes makes the Po Delta a truly unique destination.

For those who enjoy food, the Po Delta offers a chance to taste some local specialties. The region is known for its eel dishes, which are a traditional part of the local cuisine. You'll also find plenty of fresh seafood, as well as dishes made with local rice, which is grown in the fertile fields surrounding the delta. Dining in one of the small, family-run restaurants in the area is a wonderful way to experience the flavors of the region and enjoy a meal in a relaxed, friendly atmosphere.

Getting to the Po Delta is relatively easy. The region is accessible by car, with several entry points depending on where you're coming from. If you're traveling from Venice, it's about a two-hour drive to reach the heart of the delta. Once you're there, having a car is useful for exploring the more remote areas, although many of the main attractions are close together and can be reached by bike or on foot.

The Po Delta is a place of quiet beauty and natural wonder. Whether you're exploring by boat, bike, or on foot, you'll be surrounded by the tranquility of the wetlands and the rich biodiversity that makes this area so special. It's a perfect destination for a day trip or a longer stay, offering a peaceful retreat where you can reconnect with nature and discover a different side of Italy.

CHAPTER 10.
VENETIAN CUISINE

Traditional Venetian Dishes You Must Try

When you visit Venice, the city's cuisine is something you absolutely cannot miss. Venetian dishes are deeply rooted in the history and culture of the lagoon, offering a unique blend of flavors that reflect the city's maritime heritage. Here are five traditional Venetian dishes you must try, each one offering a taste of the authentic flavors that make Venice so special.

1. Sarde in Saor
One of the most iconic dishes of Venice, Sarde in Saor is a simple yet flavorful dish of fried sardines marinated in a sweet and sour mixture of onions, vinegar, pine nuts, and raisins. This dish dates back to the days when Venetian sailors needed food that would keep well on long voyages. The first time I tried Sarde in Saor, I was struck by the contrast between the tangy vinegar and the sweetness of the onions and raisins. The sardines were tender, with a slight crispness from the frying. It was a revelatory experience, as I'd never tasted anything quite like it before—both refreshing and satisfying.

2. Risotto al Nero di Seppia
Risotto al Nero di Seppia, or black squid ink risotto, is a striking dish both visually and in flavor. The ink gives the risotto its deep, black color and a rich, briny taste that is surprisingly smooth. My first encounter with this dish was memorable for its intensity. The taste was both earthy and marine, with a creamy texture that was perfectly

complemented by the hint of the sea from the squid ink. I found it fascinating how a dish so simple could offer such depth and complexity.

3. Bigoli in Salsa

Bigoli in Salsa is a classic Venetian pasta dish made with thick, whole wheat noodles called bigoli, tossed in a sauce of onions and salted fish, typically sardines or anchovies. When I first tried Bigoli in Salsa, the robust flavor of the salty fish paired with the sweetness of the onions was a delightful surprise. The pasta itself was hearty, with a texture that allowed the sauce to cling to every strand. It's a comforting dish that feels like a warm embrace, perfect after a day exploring the winding streets of Venice.

4. Fegato alla Veneziana

Fegato alla Veneziana, or Venetian-style liver, is a dish that showcases the city's love for bold flavors. The liver is sautéed with onions and typically served with polenta. I was hesitant at first, as liver can be quite strong, but this dish won me over. The liver was tender and rich, but the sweetness of the caramelized onions balanced it beautifully. Paired with the creamy polenta, it was a comforting and deeply satisfying meal that felt both rustic and refined.

5. Baccalà Mantecato

Baccalà Mantecato is a Venetian specialty made from dried codfish that is rehydrated, whipped with olive oil, and served as a creamy spread. It's often eaten on slices of toasted bread or polenta. My first taste of Baccalà Mantecato was at a small osteria near the Rialto Bridge. The texture was silky and light, with a delicate fish flavor that was both fresh and slightly salty. It was so simple yet incredibly elegant—a perfect example of how Venetian cuisine makes the most of humble ingredients.

Health Tips
When enjoying Venetian cuisine, it's important to consider any dietary restrictions or allergies. For those with gluten sensitivity, dishes like Bigoli in Salsa and Risotto al Nero di Seppia are typically made with wheat-based pasta and rice, so it's wise to ask for gluten-free options or alternatives. If you have a seafood allergy, dishes like Sarde in Saor, Risotto al Nero di Seppia, and Baccalà Mantecato should be avoided, as they all prominently feature fish or seafood. Venetian cuisine also makes frequent use of onions and vinegar, especially in dishes like Sarde in Saor, which may not be suitable for those with sensitivities to these ingredients. Always ask the restaurant staff about the ingredients used, as they are usually accommodating and can suggest alternatives that suit your dietary needs.

Venetian cuisine offers a rich tapestry of flavors that reflect the city's unique history and culture. Each dish provides a different glimpse into the life of Venice, from the salty air of the lagoon to the bustling markets filled with fresh produce. As you explore the culinary delights of Venice, don't hesitate to try something new—you might just discover a new favorite dish that captures the essence of this magical city.

Best Restaurants in Venice

Venice is a city that has captivated travelers for centuries, and its culinary scene is just as enchanting as its canals and historic architecture. The city is known for its fresh seafood, traditional Venetian dishes, and innovative cuisine that blends the old with the new. Here's a detailed guide to some of the best restaurants in Venice, each offering a unique dining experience that you shouldn't miss.

1. Antiche Carampane

Tucked away in the quiet San Polo district, Antiche Carampane is a hidden gem beloved by locals. The atmosphere here is cozy and intimate, with rustic wooden beams and walls adorned with Venetian memorabilia. This is the kind of place where you feel like you've stepped into a traditional Venetian home. The restaurant is casual yet offers a sense of old-world elegance, making it perfect for a relaxed evening with friends or a romantic dinner. Prices are moderate, with appetizers typically costing around €12-18, main courses €20-30, and desserts €8-12. Their signature dish, "Sarde in Saor," is a must-try, featuring sweet and sour marinated sardines with onions, raisins, and pine nuts. The seafood here is incredibly fresh, and their homemade pasta dishes, like "Bigoli in Salsa," are not to be missed.

2. Ristorante Alle Testiere

Located near Campo Santa Maria Formosa, Ristorante Alle Testiere is a small, upscale restaurant that has gained a reputation as one of Venice's finest dining spots. With only a handful of tables, the atmosphere is intimate and refined, making it an ideal choice for a special occasion. The decor is simple yet elegant, allowing the focus to remain on the exquisite food. Prices here are on the higher side, with appetizers ranging from €20-30, main courses €30-50, and desserts €12-15. The menu changes daily based on the freshest catch of the day, but their "Spaghetti alle Vongole" (spaghetti with clams) is a standout, prepared with a delicate touch that lets the flavors of the sea shine through. For dessert, the "Zabaione," a rich and creamy egg custard, is a delightful way to end your meal.

3. Osteria Enoteca Ai Artisti

Situated in the Dorsoduro district, Osteria Enoteca Ai Artisti is a charming, family-friendly eatery known for its warm hospitality and authentic Venetian dishes. The atmosphere here is lively yet relaxed, with a rustic interior that makes you feel at home. It's an excellent spot for a leisurely lunch or a casual dinner. Prices are reasonable, with appetizers costing around €10-15, main courses €18-25, and desserts €6-10. The "Fegato alla Veneziana," a traditional Venetian liver dish cooked with onions, is a must-try for those looking to experience authentic local flavors. Their wine selection is also impressive, with a focus on regional wines that pair beautifully with the food.

4. Il Ridotto

For those seeking an upscale dining experience, Il Ridotto is a Michelin-starred restaurant located near St. Mark's Square. The atmosphere is sophisticated and modern, with an elegant, minimalist design that creates a serene dining environment. It's perfect for a romantic evening or a celebration. Prices are on the higher end, with tasting menus ranging from €100-150 per person, but the experience is well worth it. The restaurant is known for its innovative approach to Venetian cuisine, with dishes like "Risotto al Nero di Seppia" (black squid ink risotto) and "Fritto Misto" (a mixed seafood fry) showcasing the chef's creativity and skill. The ingredients are meticulously sourced, and the presentation is nothing short of artful.

5. Trattoria da Fiore
Located in the heart of Venice, Trattoria da Fiore is a beloved local institution that offers a taste of traditional Venetian cuisine in a lively, bustling setting. The atmosphere is casual and welcoming, making it a great spot for a relaxed meal after a day of exploring the city. Prices are moderate, with appetizers around €12-20, main courses €18-28, and desserts €8-12. The "Baccalà Mantecato," a creamy codfish spread served on crostini, is a signature dish that shouldn't be missed. Their pasta dishes, such as "Tagliolini al Tartufo" (truffle tagliolini), are also highly recommended for their rich, comforting flavors.

6. Al Covo
Al Covo is a small, elegant restaurant located near the Arsenale, known for its dedication to sustainable, farm-to-table dining. The atmosphere is refined yet unpretentious, with a focus on high-quality ingredients and traditional recipes. It's an ideal spot for those who appreciate a thoughtful approach to food. Prices are on the higher side, with appetizers around €18-25, main courses €30-45, and desserts €10-15. The "Granceola," or Venetian-style spider crab, is a standout dish, showcasing the freshness of the seafood and the simplicity of Venetian cooking. Their seasonal vegetable dishes are also exceptional, offering a lighter, but equally satisfying, option.

7. Cantina Do Spade

Cantina Do Spade is one of the oldest bacari (wine bars) in Venice, located near the Rialto Market. The atmosphere here is lively and informal, with locals and tourists alike gathering to enjoy cicchetti (Venetian tapas) and a glass of wine. It's a great place for a casual bite and a drink before dinner or as a laid-back dinner option. Prices are affordable, with most cicchetti priced between €2-4 each. The "Polpette" (meatballs) and "Baccalà Mantecato" are popular choices, as well as the "Sarde in Saor," which is a classic example of Venetian cuisine at its best. The wine selection is extensive, with many local varieties to try.

8. Vecio Fritolin

Vecio Fritolin is a historic restaurant located in the Santa Croce district, known for its traditional fried dishes and seafood. The atmosphere is a blend of old and new, with a modern interior that pays homage to its roots as a 17th-century fritolin (a place where fried foods were sold). It's an excellent choice for those who want to experience authentic Venetian street food in a sit-down setting. Prices are moderate to high, with appetizers around €15-20, main courses €25-40, and desserts €8-12. The "Fritto Misto," a mixed fry of seafood and vegetables, is the highlight of the menu, offering a taste of Venice's deep-fried delights. Pair it with a glass of local Prosecco for a truly Venetian experience.

9. Ristorante Quadri

Overlooking St. Mark's Square, Ristorante Quadri is a luxurious dining destination that offers a spectacular view of one of Venice's most famous landmarks. The atmosphere is opulent and grand, with an interior that reflects the city's rich history and artistic heritage. It's the perfect place for a special occasion or a memorable night out. Prices are on the higher end, with tasting menus starting at €160 per person. The menu is a blend of traditional Venetian and contemporary Italian cuisine, with dishes like "Cappesante al Tartufo" (scallops with truffle) and "Agnello al Forno" (roast lamb) showcasing the finest ingredients and expert preparation. The desserts are equally impressive, with the "Tiramisù" being a standout.

10. Trattoria Corte Sconta
Hidden away in the Castello district, Trattoria Corte Sconta is a family-run restaurant that offers a true taste of Venetian hospitality. The atmosphere is warm and inviting, with a charming courtyard that's perfect for dining al fresco in the warmer months. It's a popular spot with locals, making it a great place to experience authentic Venetian cuisine. Prices are moderate, with appetizers around €10-15, main courses €20-30, and desserts €6-10. The seafood here is exceptional, with the "Antipasto di Mare" (seafood antipasto) being a must-try for its variety and freshness. The homemade pasta dishes are also a highlight, with the "Spaghetti alla Busara" (spaghetti with scampi) being particularly delicious.

Venice's dining scene is as diverse and captivating as the city itself, offering everything from simple, traditional dishes to innovative, gourmet experiences. Whether you're in the mood for a casual meal in a local osteria or a luxurious dinner overlooking the Grand Canal, Venice has something to satisfy every palate. As you explore the city, take the time to enjoy its culinary delights—you'll discover that the food is just as much a part of Venice's charm as its canals and palaces.

Wine Bars and Bacari: Venetian Tapas Culture

Venice has a unique and vibrant food culture that is deeply intertwined with its history and lifestyle. One of the most delightful ways to experience Venetian cuisine is through its wine bars and bacari, which are small, casual places where you can enjoy a drink and sample various small bites known as cicchetti. This tradition of enjoying food and wine in a relaxed, social setting is a beloved part of everyday life in Venice, and it's something that every visitor should experience.

Bacari are cozy, unpretentious spots often found tucked away in the narrow streets of Venice. They're usually quite small, with just a few tables or even just a bar counter where locals and visitors alike gather to enjoy a glass of wine or a spritz (a popular Venetian cocktail made with prosecco, Aperol or Campari, and a splash of soda water). What makes bacari special, though, is the selection of cicchetti they offer. These are small plates or snacks that are similar to Spanish tapas and are perfect for sharing.

Cicchetti can vary widely depending on the bar and the season, but you'll often find classics like crostini topped with baccalà mantecato (creamed salt cod), slices of cured meats, marinated seafood, meatballs (polpette), and fried vegetables. The portions are small, making it easy to try several different things, and they're usually priced affordably, allowing you to sample a variety of flavors without breaking the bank. This is a great way to immerse yourself in the local food scene, tasting a little bit of everything while enjoying the lively atmosphere.

One of the best things about bacari is their laid-back vibe. These are not fancy restaurants but rather places where you can drop in for a quick snack and a drink, chat with the bartender or other patrons, and soak up the authentic Venetian atmosphere. The setting is often rustic, with wooden beams, old wine barrels, and simple décor that gives you a sense of stepping back in time.

Some of the most popular bacari in Venice include Cantina Do Mori, which claims to be one of the oldest wine bars in the city, dating back to the 15th century. Here, you can enjoy a glass of wine surrounded by historical charm, with hanging copper pots and vintage photographs adding to the ambiance. Their selection of cicchetti is impressive, offering traditional options like artichoke hearts, stuffed peppers, and anchovies on toast.

Another favorite is Al Bottegon (Cantine del Vino già Schiavi), a family-run bacaro near the Accademia Bridge. This spot is particularly known for its wide variety of crostini topped with everything from smoked fish to truffle cream. It's a great place to stop in for a glass of wine and a few bites while exploring the Dorsoduro district.

For a more contemporary take on the bacaro tradition, visit Osteria al Squero, which is located along a picturesque canal in the Dorsoduro area. It's a popular spot with students and young locals, offering a lively atmosphere and a wide selection of wines by the glass. Their cicchetti are fresh and flavorful, featuring seasonal ingredients and modern twists on classic dishes.

Another must-visit is Cantina Do Spade, near the Rialto Market. This bacaro is steeped in history, with roots dating back to the 15th century. It's a lively spot where you can try some of the best cicchetti in Venice, such as polpette (meatballs), sarde in saor (sweet and sour sardines), and small sandwiches filled with prosciutto or cheese.

When visiting these wine bars and bacari, it's important to keep in mind that the atmosphere is casual and the service is often self-serve, especially when it comes to the cicchetti. You typically order at the bar, select your food, and then either stand at a counter or find a small table to enjoy your meal. This informal style is part of the charm and allows you to experience Venice like a local.

If you have dietary restrictions or allergies, it's always a good idea to ask about the ingredients before ordering. Many cicchetti are made with fresh seafood, which can be a concern for those with shellfish allergies. Gluten-free options might be limited, as many dishes are served on bread or involve fried items. However, there are usually a few options that can accommodate different dietary needs, such as grilled vegetables or dishes served without bread.

Exploring the wine bars and bacari of Venice is not just about the food and drink; it's about immersing yourself in a way of life that has been cherished by Venetians for generations. It's about slowing down, savoring the flavors, and enjoying good company in a beautiful, historic setting. Whether you're hopping from one bacaro to another or settling in at a favorite spot, this is an experience that captures the true essence of Venice.

Venice's Food Markets: Rialto Market and More

Venice is a city that comes alive with the colors, smells, and sounds of its bustling food markets. The most famous of these is the Rialto Market, but there are other local markets that offer a glimpse into the everyday life of Venetians and a taste of the region's fresh, seasonal produce. Exploring these markets is a sensory experience that shouldn't be missed.

The Rialto Market is at the heart of Venice, near the iconic Rialto Bridge. For centuries, it has been the city's main marketplace, and it remains a lively hub of activity today. The market is divided into two sections: the Pescheria, where you'll find an incredible array of fresh seafood, and the Erberia, which is filled with stalls selling fruits, vegetables, and other local products.

The Pescheria is a feast for the eyes and the palate. As you wander through the stalls, you'll see fishmongers displaying their catch of the day, from glistening fish to octopus, squid, and shellfish. The variety is impressive, and it's a great place to learn about the local seafood that plays such a big role in Venetian cuisine. Even if you're not planning to cook, it's worth visiting just to take in the sights and smells and to watch the locals as they pick out the freshest ingredients for their meals.

In the Erberia section, the market is filled with vibrant fruits and vegetables. Depending on the season, you'll find everything from juicy tomatoes and zucchini flowers to wild mushrooms and artichokes. Many of the vendors sell produce grown in the nearby islands of the Venetian lagoon, such as Sant'Erasmo, which is known as the "vegetable garden" of Venice. These local products are full of flavor, and it's fascinating to see what's in season during your visit.

One of the best things about the Rialto Market is the atmosphere. The market is busiest in the mornings when locals come to do their shopping, and there's a lively energy as vendors call out their prices and customers haggle over the best deals. It's a great place to soak up the local culture and get a sense of the daily rhythms of life in Venice.

While the Rialto Market is the most famous, it's not the only food market in Venice. If you venture off the beaten path, you'll find smaller, more local markets in different neighborhoods. For example, the Campo Santa Margherita market in the Dorsoduro district is a charming spot where you can find fresh produce, cheese, and meats. It's a bit quieter and more relaxed than the Rialto, making it a great place to shop if you're staying in the area.

Another market worth visiting is the Mercato di San Leonardo in the Cannaregio district. This market is less touristy and more frequented by locals, offering a more authentic shopping experience. Here, you can find fresh fruits and vegetables, as well as local delicacies like cured meats and cheeses. It's a lovely place to explore if you're interested in seeing a different side of Venice.

If you're a food lover, exploring Venice's markets is a must-do activity. Not only do you get to see and taste some of the freshest ingredients in the city, but you also get a sense of the deep connection Venetians have with their food and their land. The markets are places where tradition meets daily life, and they offer a window into the rich culinary heritage of the region.

When visiting the markets, it's a good idea to go early in the morning when the selection is at its best and the atmosphere is most lively. Most markets start winding down by midday, so plan to arrive around 8 or 9 AM to see them at their peak. If you're planning to buy anything, especially seafood, be prepared to carry it with you as refrigeration might not be available.

If you have any dietary restrictions, the markets are a great place to find fresh ingredients that meet your needs. However, it's always a good idea to ask the vendors about how certain items are prepared or sourced, especially if you have specific allergies or preferences.

Exploring Venice's food markets is a delightful way to experience the city's culture and flavors. Whether you're buying ingredients for a picnic, looking for a unique souvenir, or simply enjoying the atmosphere, these markets offer a taste of Venice that you won't find anywhere else.

Cooking Classes and Food Tours

Experiencing the culinary delights of Venice isn't just about dining out; it's also about getting hands-on with the ingredients and techniques that make Venetian cuisine so special. Cooking classes and food tours offer a wonderful way to immerse yourself in the city's rich culinary traditions. Whether you're a seasoned cook or a complete beginner, these experiences are designed to be fun, informative, and, of course, delicious.

One of the best ways to dive into Venetian cooking is by taking a cooking class with a local chef. These classes often start with a visit to the Rialto Market, where you'll pick out fresh ingredients for the dishes you'll be preparing. The market visit alone is a fascinating experience, as your chef guides you through the stalls, explaining the seasonal produce and local seafood that are the heart of Venetian cuisine. You'll learn how to select the best fish, vegetables, and other ingredients while gaining insight into the traditions that have shaped the city's food culture.

Back in the kitchen, the cooking class begins. Most classes are held in small groups, ensuring that everyone gets personalized attention. You'll learn how to prepare classic Venetian dishes such as risotto, fresh pasta, and seafood dishes like sarde in saor (sweet and sour sardines). The chef will share tips and techniques that have been passed down through generations, giving you a real taste of how Venetians cook at home.

One of the highlights of these classes is the opportunity to enjoy the fruits of your labor. After a few hours of cooking, you'll sit down with your fellow participants to enjoy the meal you've prepared, paired with local wines. It's a satisfying and social way to end the experience, and you'll leave with new skills and recipes to recreate at home.

If you're more interested in tasting than cooking, a food tour is an excellent way to explore Venice's culinary scene. Led by knowledgeable guides, these tours take you on a journey through the city's best eateries, from hidden bacari (Venetian wine bars) to family-run trattorias. You'll sample a variety of Venetian specialties, such as cicchetti (small plates), fresh seafood, and traditional desserts like tiramisu.

Food tours often include stops at local markets, bakeries, and artisan shops, where you can taste everything from freshly baked bread to artisanal gelato. Along the way, your guide will share stories about the history of Venetian cuisine, the significance of certain dishes, and the cultural traditions that continue to influence the city's food today. It's a great way to learn about Venice while indulging in its culinary delights.

For those with dietary restrictions, many cooking classes and food tours offer options to accommodate your needs. It's always a good idea to let the organizers know about any allergies or preferences when you book, so they can tailor the experience to ensure you have a safe and enjoyable time.

Whether you choose a cooking class or a food tour, these experiences offer a deeper connection to Venice's food culture. They provide a unique opportunity to learn from locals, discover hidden culinary gems, and taste the authentic flavors of the city. Beyond the food itself, these activities offer a way to engage with the traditions and stories that make Venetian cuisine so rich and rewarding.

Taking part in a cooking class or food tour in Venice is more than just a chance to eat well; it's an opportunity to understand the city's culinary soul. You'll leave with memories of delicious meals, new skills, and a greater appreciation for the food culture that defines this remarkable city.

Vegetarian and Vegan Dining in Venice

Venice, with its rich culinary traditions, might seem like a place dominated by seafood and meat dishes, but it also offers a variety of options for vegetarian and vegan diners. Finding delicious plant-based meals in this enchanting city is both satisfying and enjoyable, as Venice has embraced diverse dietary preferences over the years.

When you're in Venice and looking for vegetarian or vegan options, start by exploring local trattorias and restaurants that offer menus accommodating different dietary needs. Many places now feature vegetarian dishes prominently and are often willing to adapt meals to fit vegan requirements.

One standout spot is Ristorante Da Ivo, known for its welcoming atmosphere and a menu that includes both vegetarian and vegan choices. The restaurant's cozy setting makes it a pleasant place to enjoy a meal. They offer delightful dishes like risotto with seasonal vegetables and pasta with fresh, flavorful sauces that cater to vegetarian and vegan diets. It's advisable to ask the staff about vegan options, as they are usually happy to customize dishes based on dietary needs.

Another great choice is La Zucca, a charming restaurant that has become popular among those seeking vegetarian and vegan fare. The menu is thoughtfully designed, featuring a range of dishes like pumpkin risotto and vegetable lasagna. The restaurant's emphasis on fresh, local ingredients makes the meals both nutritious and tasty. Their creative approach to vegetarian and vegan cooking ensures that every dish is satisfying and full of flavor.

For a casual dining experience, consider visiting Osteria al Squero. This local gem offers a variety of cicchetti, the Venetian version of tapas, with several vegetarian options. You can enjoy small plates of marinated vegetables, crostini with vegan spreads, and salads. The relaxed vibe of the restaurant and its location near the famous Squero di San Trovaso (a historic gondola workshop) adds to the charm of dining here.

If you're looking for a place that specializes in plant-based cuisine, Veganima is a must-visit. This vegan restaurant offers a completely plant-based menu with dishes inspired by traditional Italian recipes. From hearty pasta dishes to flavorful vegan burgers, you'll find plenty of options that are both satisfying and inventive. The restaurant's focus on fresh ingredients and creative recipes makes it a popular choice for vegans and vegetarians alike.

For those who prefer to explore markets and prepare their own meals, Venice's food markets are great places to find fresh produce, bread, and other plant-based ingredients. The Rialto Market is a bustling hub where you can buy seasonal vegetables, fruits, and even vegan-friendly snacks. The market experience allows you to engage with local vendors and select ingredients for a homemade meal.

Dining out in Venice as a vegetarian or vegan can be a delightful experience if you know where to look. Many restaurants are increasingly accommodating to different dietary needs, and with a bit of exploration, you can enjoy a variety of delicious plant-based dishes. Always feel free to ask the staff about vegan options or any modifications to make a dish suitable for your dietary preferences.

Overall, Venice's dining scene offers plenty of choices for vegetarians and vegans. With a mix of dedicated vegan spots, accommodating trattorias, and fresh market options, you'll find that eating plant-based in Venice can be both enjoyable and fulfilling.

CHAPTER 11.
VENICE WITH FAMILY
Family-Friendly Attractions

Venice is a magical city for families, offering a range of attractions that cater to all ages. If you're visiting with children, you'll find plenty to keep everyone entertained while exploring the charm of this unique city.

One of the most exciting places to visit is the Venice Aquarium. Located on the island of Murano, this small but engaging aquarium is perfect for young explorers. It showcases local marine life in a way that's both educational and fun. Kids can learn about the creatures living in the Venetian lagoon and see them up close. The aquarium is easy to reach by Vaporetto (water bus), making it a convenient stop during your visit.

Another fantastic family-friendly spot is Lido Beach. This long stretch of sandy beach is a great place for children to run around and play. The calm waters are ideal for swimming, and there are several family-friendly facilities, including playgrounds and cafes. You can easily get there by Vaporetto from the main city, and it's a refreshing break from the busy streets of Venice.

For a more interactive experience, the Natural History Museum in Venice is a great choice. The museum is located in a beautiful old palace and offers fascinating exhibits that are sure to captivate kids. From dinosaur fossils to displays about local wildlife, the museum provides an engaging way for children to learn about nature and science.

If your family enjoys a bit of adventure, the Peggy Guggenheim Collection can also be an intriguing destination. While it's primarily an art museum, it's housed in a beautiful palace with lovely gardens. The artwork and sculptures might spark the imagination of older children, and the gardens are a pleasant place to explore and relax.

A unique way to see Venice is by taking a Gondola Ride. While it's a bit of a splurge, it's a quintessential Venetian experience that children often find magical. Gliding along the canals and seeing the city from the water can be an unforgettable experience for the whole family. There are various gondola services throughout the city, and many offer shorter, more affordable rides.

For something more interactive, the Venetian Puppet Theatre offers entertaining shows that can be a hit with younger children. The performances are engaging and colorful, and they provide a glimpse into traditional Venetian culture through the art of puppetry. Shows are often held in small, cozy venues, which makes for an intimate and enjoyable experience.

Additionally, exploring the charming Piazza San Marco and its surroundings can be fun for families. The piazza is a lively place where children can enjoy watching the pigeons, listening to live music, and even visiting the nearby Doge's Palace if they are interested in history and grandeur. The square itself is spacious and provides a nice area for kids to wander around.

When visiting Venice with children, keep in mind that the city's narrow streets and canals can be quite crowded. It's a good idea to take frequent breaks and keep hydrated. Many restaurants and cafes are family-friendly, so you'll have no trouble finding a place to relax and refuel.

Venice offers a variety of family-friendly attractions that make it a wonderful destination for travelers with children. From educational experiences to relaxing beach outings and interactive adventures, there's something to delight every member of the family.

Activities for Kids in Venice

Venice is a city filled with wonder for kids, offering a mix of fun activities that will keep the whole family entertained. Here are some great activities to consider:

A gondola ride is a classic Venetian experience that kids often find magical. As you glide along the canals, you'll see the city from a unique perspective. It's a relaxing and exciting way for children to experience Venice. Many gondolas are equipped with comfortable seats, and the ride itself is a smooth and enjoyable experience. Just remember to book in advance if you're visiting during peak times.

The Venice Lido Beach is another fantastic spot for families. This beach offers plenty of space for kids to run around and play. The sand is perfect for building castles, and the shallow waters are safe for swimming. There are also playgrounds and snack bars nearby, making it a convenient place for a family day out. You can get there easily by Vaporetto from the main city.

For a bit of adventure, consider visiting the Venice Aquarium on the island of Murano. It's a small, engaging aquarium that showcases local marine life. Kids can see various fish and other sea creatures that live in the Venetian lagoon. The aquarium is both educational and fun, offering an exciting way for children to learn about the aquatic world.

Exploring the Natural History Museum in Venice is another great option. The museum is located in a beautiful old building and features fascinating exhibits that are sure to capture kids' imaginations. From dinosaur skeletons to displays on local wildlife, the museum provides an interactive and educational experience. The exhibits are well designed to be interesting for children and adults alike.

The Peggy Guggenheim Collection, while primarily an art museum, is housed in a lovely palace with beautiful gardens. It's a great place for a leisurely stroll. Children may enjoy the colorful modern art and the chance to explore the gardens, where they can run around and see sculptures. The museum's setting makes for a pleasant outing.

The Venetian Puppet Theatre offers entertaining shows that can be a hit with younger children. The puppet performances are lively and engaging, providing a glimpse into traditional Venetian entertainment. It's a fun way for kids to experience local culture in an interactive manner.

Piazza San Marco, the main square in Venice, is another spot that kids will enjoy. The large open space is perfect for running around, and the piazza is home to beautiful buildings and street performers. Watching the pigeons is a simple pleasure that kids often love. The nearby cafes and restaurants offer plenty of places to rest and have a snack.

For a bit of hands-on fun, consider taking a glass-blowing workshop on the island of Murano. Many studios offer short, family-friendly sessions where kids can learn about the art of glass-making. It's a unique experience that allows children to see artisans at work and even try their hand at making something.

Finally, wandering through the narrow streets and over the many bridges of Venice can be an adventure in itself. Kids will enjoy exploring and discovering hidden corners of the city. Make sure to stop for gelato breaks – the sweet treat is a favorite among children and a great way to cool off.

Venice is full of activities that cater to children's interests and energy levels. From gondola rides and beach outings to museums and puppet shows, there's plenty to keep kids entertained and make your visit enjoyable for the whole family.

Tips for Traveling with Children

Traveling with children in Venice can be a delightful experience with a bit of planning and preparation. Here are some tips to help make your trip smooth and enjoyable.

Start by preparing for the unique logistics of Venice. The city is famous for its canals and narrow streets, which means you won't find cars here. Instead, you'll be using boats and walking a lot. Make sure to pack comfortable shoes for everyone. Strollers can be challenging on the cobblestone streets, so consider bringing a lightweight, foldable stroller that's easy to carry.

When it comes to accommodation, choose a place that is centrally located. This makes it easier to get to popular attractions without having to travel long distances. Many hotels and rentals in Venice are family-friendly and offer amenities like cribs or extra beds. Check in advance to ensure your accommodation can cater to your needs.

Plan your activities keeping your children's interests and energy levels in mind. Venice has many attractions, but it's wise to mix up sightseeing with downtime. Include some playgrounds or open spaces in your itinerary where kids can play and burn off energy. The Venice Lido Beach and some parks in the city are perfect for this.

If you're visiting popular sites like St. Mark's Basilica or the Doge's Palace, be prepared for lines and crowds. It's helpful to book tickets in advance when possible to avoid long waits.

Also, consider visiting attractions early in the morning or later in the afternoon to avoid peak times.

Keep your children entertained during longer waits or boat rides. Bring along small toys, coloring books, or electronic devices to keep them engaged. Having snacks on hand can also be a lifesaver for keeping little ones happy and satisfied.

Venice's dining options are generally family-friendly, but it's a good idea to check menus in advance if your children have specific dietary needs. Many restaurants offer high chairs and are accommodating to families. Local gelato shops are a hit with kids and provide a nice treat during your explorations.

Staying hydrated and keeping your children's energy up is important. Make sure to carry water bottles and snacks while exploring. Many restaurants and shops provide water refills, so you don't need to carry too much at once.

Safety is always a top priority. Venice is a safe city, but always keep an eye on your children, especially near water or busy areas. Make sure they understand basic safety rules and are aware of their surroundings.

Enjoy the experience and be flexible. Traveling with children can sometimes be unpredictable, so it's important to stay adaptable and go with the flow. Venice is a beautiful city with lots to offer, and your family will make wonderful memories exploring it together.

With a bit of planning and these tips in mind, your family trip to Venice will be an unforgettable adventure for everyone.

Best Places to Eat with Kids

Finding the right places to eat with kids in Venice can make your family dining experience enjoyable and stress-free. Here are some of the best places to consider:

For a casual and family-friendly meal, Pizzeria Da Michele is a great choice. Located at Salizzada San Lio, 5706, this spot offers a relaxed atmosphere with delicious, simple pizzas that kids love. The menu features classic options like Margherita and Pepperoni, and the staff is welcoming to families. The restaurant is easy to find and centrally located, making it a convenient stop during your day of sightseeing.

Another excellent option is Osteria Al Squero, situated at Dorsoduro 2727. This charming eatery serves traditional Venetian dishes in a casual setting. They offer a variety of pasta and seafood dishes, but the kid-friendly options like pasta with tomato sauce are a hit with younger diners. The outdoor seating area is a nice spot to enjoy a meal while watching the gondolas pass by.

If your family enjoys a bit of variety, Bacaro Risorto at Santa Croce 1467 provides a wide range of options from Venetian tapas to pizza. The casual, relaxed atmosphere and friendly staff make it a comfortable place for families. Kids will enjoy the variety of small dishes, and there are also plenty of non-seafood options available.

For a treat that kids will love, Gelateria Nico on Fondamenta Zattere 922 is a must-visit. This gelato shop is famous for its creamy, delicious ice cream and offers a wide range of flavors.

It's a perfect stop for a sweet break while exploring the city. The shop has a casual vibe, and the staff is happy to help with flavor choices.

Rosticceria Gislon, located at Campo S. Bartolomeo, 5184, is known for its quick, tasty meals that are great for kids. They offer a range of traditional Venetian dishes, including sandwiches and small plates, making it easy to grab a meal on the go. The relaxed atmosphere and simple menu make it a good choice for families looking for a straightforward dining experience.

Each of these spots provides a family-friendly atmosphere with options that cater to children's tastes, making your dining experiences in Venice enjoyable and stress-free.

CHAPTER 12.
PRACTICAL INFORMATION

Currency And Payments

When planning a trip to Venice, understanding how to manage your money can make your experience smoother and more enjoyable. Here's a guide to help you navigate currency exchange, payment methods, and budgeting effectively.

In Venice, the currency used is the Euro (€). This is the same currency used throughout Italy and much of the Eurozone. The Euro is widely accepted and is essential for all your transactions, whether you're shopping for souvenirs or dining in a local restaurant.

For currency exchange, you have several options. Banks are reliable places to exchange currency, and they often offer competitive rates. You can find them throughout Venice, with the major branches being easily identifiable in the city center. Currency exchange offices, or "Cambio" shops, are also prevalent and can be found near tourist areas such as Piazza San Marco and the Rialto Bridge. These offices may charge a fee or offer slightly less favorable rates, so it's a good idea to compare a few options if you have the time. ATMs are another convenient option for obtaining Euros, and they are widely available throughout the city. However, be aware that your bank might charge a foreign transaction fee, and the ATM might offer an exchange rate that is not as favorable. To avoid high fees, it's best to withdraw larger amounts less frequently.

When it comes to budgeting, Venice can cater to various travel styles. For budget travelers, expect to spend around €70-€100 per day, including accommodation in hostels or budget hotels, simple meals, and public transportation. Mid-range travelers might spend between €150-€250 per day, which would cover stays in comfortable hotels or B&Bs, dining in a mix of casual and nicer restaurants, and entrance fees to various attractions. Luxury travelers could easily spend €300 or more per day, enjoying high-end hotels, fine dining, private tours, and exclusive experiences.

Credit and debit cards are widely accepted in Venice, especially in larger establishments such as hotels, restaurants, and shops. Visa and Mastercard are the most commonly accepted cards, while American Express may be less widely accepted. It's a good idea to carry some cash, as smaller shops, local markets, and some eateries may not accept cards or might prefer cash transactions.

Pricing in Venice can vary significantly. Tourist hotspots like Piazza San Marco and the Grand Canal tend to have higher prices, both for dining and shopping. For more budget-friendly options, explore areas like the Cannaregio or Dorsoduro neighborhoods. Seasonal variations also affect costs; visiting during peak tourist seasons like summer and major holidays can lead to higher prices. Be aware of hidden costs such as service charges or cover charges at some restaurants.

Reflecting on my own experience, I remember struggling a bit with finding the best currency exchange rates when I first arrived in Venice. After exchanging a small amount at the airport, I quickly realized that the rates were much better at local exchange offices. I also found it handy to have a budgeting app on my phone to keep track of expenses and make sure I stayed within my daily budget.

To manage your finances effectively, consider using budgeting apps like Mint or YNAB (You Need A Budget) to keep track of your spending. Currency converter apps, such as XE Currency, can help you monitor exchange rates and convert prices on the go. Websites like TripAdvisor and Yelp can also provide insights into local pricing trends and help you find the best deals.

With this guide, you'll be better prepared to handle money matters during your trip to Venice, ensuring that you can enjoy the city's beauty without financial stress.

Language Tips for Travelers

When visiting Venice, understanding the basics of the local languages can greatly enhance your travel experience. The primary language spoken in Venice is Italian, as it is throughout Italy. Additionally, given Venice's historical connections and its location, German is also spoken by some locals and is used in certain contexts, especially in tourism.

Italian is essential for most interactions, while German might come in handy in specific tourist areas. Venetian dialects and regional variations do exist, but most locals will understand and appreciate your efforts to use standard Italian.

For basic greetings and polite phrases in Italian, here are some essentials:
- Hello: Ciao (chow) or Salve (SAHL-veh) - Use "Ciao" informally and "Salve" in more formal settings.
- Please: Per favore (per fah-VOH-ray)
- Thank you: Grazie (GRAHTS-ee-eh)
- Excuse me: Scusi (SKOO-zee) - Use this when you need to get someone's attention or apologize.

If you need to use German, here are some key phrases:
- Hello: Hallo (HAH-loh)
- Please: Bitte (BIT-teh)
- Thank you: Danke (DAHN-keh)
- Excuse me: Entschuldigung (ent-SHUL-dee-goong)

For practical phrases to use in various situations:
- Ordering food:

- Italian: "Vorrei ordinare..." (vohr-REH-ee or-dee-NAH-ray) - "I would like to order..."
    - German: "Ich möchte bestellen..." (ikh MOHCH-teh beh-SHTEL-len) - "I would like to order..."

- Asking for directions:
    - Italian: "Dove si trova...?" (DOH-veh see TROH-vah) - "Where is...?"
    - German: "Wo befindet sich...?" (voh beh-FIN-det zikh) - "Where is...?"

- Making purchases:
    - Italian: "Quanto costa?" (KWAHN-toh KOH-stah) - "How much does it cost?"
    - German: "Wie viel kostet das?" (vee feel KOH-stet dahs) - "How much does it cost?"

- Seeking assistance:
    - Italian: "Può aiutarmi?" (PWOH ah-yoo-TAR-mee) - "Can you help me?"
    - German: "Können Sie mir bitte helfen?" (KEU-nen zee meer BIT-teh HEL-fen) - "Can you help me, please?"

To help you learn these phrases, consider using language learning resources like phrasebooks or mobile apps. Apps such as Duolingo, Babbel, or Google Translate can be particularly useful for quickly picking up essential phrases. Online tutorials on platforms like YouTube also offer pronunciation guides and basic language lessons tailored to travelers.

Culturally, Italians appreciate it when visitors make an effort to speak their language. Using formal language, like "Buongiorno" (Good morning) or "Buonasera" (Good evening), when addressing people you don't know is considered polite. In informal settings, such as with friends or younger people, "Ciao" is perfectly acceptable.

In tourist areas, many locals, especially those working in hotels, restaurants, and major attractions, speak English. Look for signs indicating English-speaking staff or simply ask if someone can assist you in English. However, making an effort with the local language is always valued and shows respect for the local culture.

Understanding and using basic Italian phrases not only helps you navigate Venice more smoothly but also demonstrates a respectful attitude toward the local community. Embrace the opportunity to connect with Venetians through their language, and you'll find that your interactions become much richer and more rewarding.

Health and Safety in Venice

When planning a trip to Venice, staying safe and healthy is crucial to fully enjoying your visit. Here's a guide to help you navigate safety and health considerations in this beautiful city.

General Safety Tips

Venice is generally a safe city, but it's wise to remain aware of your surroundings as you explore its charming canals and narrow streets. Always keep an eye on your belongings, especially in crowded areas or popular tourist spots where pickpocketing can occur. Avoid poorly lit or secluded areas, particularly at night. When navigating the city's labyrinth of alleys, it's helpful to have a map or GPS device to prevent getting lost. Respect local customs and regulations, such as dress codes in religious sites, to ensure a smooth and respectful visit.

Outdoor Safety

While Venice itself is relatively flat and lacks mountainous terrain, outdoor safety becomes more relevant when you venture to nearby regions or engage in activities like hiking or skiing in the surrounding areas. Always check weather conditions before heading out, as sudden changes can impact your plans. For hiking, ensure you understand trail markers and start early in the day to avoid getting caught after dark. If you plan to ski, be aware of altitude sickness symptoms, such as headaches and dizziness, and take it easy to acclimate.

Health Precautions

Staying healthy in Venice involves a few straightforward practices. Keep hydrated, particularly if you're walking a lot in the summer heat. Use sunscreen to protect yourself from the strong sun, even on cloudy days. The weather can change rapidly, so dress in layers to stay comfortable throughout the day. While there are no specific vaccinations required for visiting Venice, it's always a good idea to be up to date with routine vaccinations.

Emergency Contacts

In case of emergencies, you can call 112 for general emergency services, which will connect you to police, fire, or medical assistance. For specific medical emergencies, you might need to visit one of Venice's hospitals or clinics. The Ospedale Civile di Venezia, located at Cannaregio 23, is the primary hospital in Venice. For outdoor rescue services, especially if you venture into more remote areas, contacting local guides or rescue organizations is crucial. Always have a local contact number handy, such as your hotel or accommodation, to assist in navigating emergencies.

Travel Insurance

Before traveling, securing a comprehensive travel insurance policy is essential. Ensure your policy covers health-related issues, emergency evacuations, and medical expenses. Check for coverage that includes trip cancellations, lost baggage, and theft. It's beneficial to choose a policy with 24/7 support and global coverage to handle unexpected situations effectively.

Local Health Services

Venice is well-equipped with health services. Pharmacies are plentiful and can be found throughout the city. Many have English-speaking staff and can provide over-the-counter medications or advice. For more serious health issues, there are several clinics and hospitals, including the previously mentioned Ospedale Civile di Venezia. Many clinics also offer walk-in services for urgent care.

Resources and Tools

To stay informed and safe, consider using safety apps like Smart Traveler or local Venice apps that provide updates on health and safety conditions. Websites such as the Venice Tourism Board can offer up-to-date information on local events, safety tips, and health advisories. Carrying a portable charger for your phone is also a good idea to ensure you have access to emergency services and maps at all times.

By following these tips, you'll be well-prepared to enjoy your trip to Venice with peace of mind, knowing that you're taking the necessary steps to stay safe and healthy.

Emergency Contacts and Services

When traveling to Venice, it's crucial to be prepared for any emergencies that may arise. Here's a comprehensive guide to help you navigate emergency situations with confidence.

In Venice, emergency services are efficient and accessible, whether you're in the heart of the city or exploring its outskirts. The city provides robust police, fire, and medical services to ensure your safety. In urban areas, help is readily available, while in more rural or remote areas, it's important to know how to access these services quickly.

For any urgent situation, you can dial 112, the general emergency number throughout the European Union, including Venice. This number will connect you to police, fire services, and medical assistance. Specifically, for local police in Venice, you can call 041 274 8111. If you need an ambulance, the same general emergency number (112) will connect you to ambulance services, which are equipped to handle medical emergencies promptly. For fire emergencies, the number 115 is dedicated to fire services in Italy. If you find yourself in a mountainous or remote area requiring rescue, specialized mountain rescue services can be reached through local guides or by calling 118.

Venice has several local hospitals and clinics that cater to a range of medical needs. The Ospedale Civile di Venezia is the primary hospital located at Cannaregio 23, reachable at 041 529 4111. This hospital provides comprehensive medical care, including emergency services. For less urgent matters or specific medical needs, you can visit smaller clinics or pharmacies spread throughout the city. Pharmacies, or "farmacie," are numerous and often have English-speaking staff.

In case of an emergency, it's important to stay calm and communicate clearly. Provide your location, describe the nature of the emergency, and any relevant details about your situation. If you're not fluent in Italian, having a basic understanding of key phrases or using translation apps can be very helpful. Emergency responders are accustomed to dealing with tourists and will assist you as needed.

Travel insurance is highly recommended for any trip, and this is particularly true for Venice. Ensure your policy covers medical emergencies, evacuation, and other unforeseen issues. Many insurance companies offer 24/7 assistance services that can help you navigate emergencies abroad. Keep your insurance details and emergency contact numbers handy, and familiarize yourself with how to contact your insurance provider for immediate help.

For outdoor activities such as hiking or exploring remote areas, preparation is key. Always carry a first aid kit, inform someone of your plans, and check the weather forecast before heading out. If you're venturing into areas known for hiking or skiing, make sure to follow safety guidelines and be aware of any potential hazards.

Culturally, Venetians are generally helpful and polite. When seeking assistance, approaching locals with courtesy and a smile can go a long way. If you need help, asking in English is usually fine, as many Venetians speak it, especially in tourist areas. Showing appreciation for their assistance will be well-received.

Reflecting on a personal experience, I recall a time when a fellow traveler had a minor accident while exploring the nearby islands. They needed medical attention quickly, and knowing the emergency numbers and having their insurance details ready made a significant difference. The local responders were efficient, and their insurance provider offered immediate support, highlighting the importance of preparation and knowing the local systems.

To stay informed and prepared, consider downloading emergency apps that provide local information and safety updates. Websites like the Venice Tourism Board also offer resources that can help you understand local emergency protocols and health services.

By being well-prepared and aware of these emergency resources, you can ensure a safer and more enjoyable trip to Venice.

Accessible Venice: Tips for Travelers with Disabilities

Traveling to Venice can be an enchanting experience, and with a bit of planning, it's also possible to enjoy the city even if you have disabilities. Venice is known for its charming canals and historic buildings, but navigating its unique layout requires some consideration. Here's a guide to help make your visit as smooth and enjoyable as possible.

Venice's compact and historic streets present some challenges, particularly for those using wheelchairs or mobility aids. The city is renowned for its canals and bridges, and many of these bridges have steps, which can be a hurdle. However, the city has been working to improve accessibility. Many of the main tourist areas and attractions have accessible paths and facilities. Public transportation, such as Vaporetto water buses, has services designed for those with mobility issues.

To get around the city, you'll find that some Vaporetto lines, especially those operated by ACTV, have low-floor boats that are wheelchair accessible. The key lines to look out for are Line 1, which travels along the Grand Canal, and Line 4.1 and 4.2, which provide connections between different parts of the city. Be sure to check the latest information on accessibility before you travel, as services can vary.

For those staying overnight, many hotels in Venice have adapted to accommodate guests with disabilities. It's a good idea to contact hotels directly to inquire about their facilities, such as accessible rooms, ramps, and elevators. Some hotels are located in historic buildings, which might have limited accessibility, so confirming these details in advance will help ensure a comfortable stay.

Restaurants and cafes in Venice are increasingly accommodating to guests with disabilities. Many have ground-level entrances or ramps, though it's always wise to check in advance. The larger, more modern establishments are generally better equipped with accessible facilities. When in doubt, don't hesitate to call ahead and ask about accessibility features.

The main tourist attractions, like St. Mark's Basilica and the Doge's Palace, have made strides in becoming more accessible. St. Mark's Basilica, for instance, offers guided tours that are adapted for wheelchair users. The Doge's Palace has ramps and elevators to help visitors navigate its many floors. However, because these historic sites can be challenging due to their age and design, contacting them in advance to confirm the availability of accessibility services can be beneficial.

Venice also has several parks and open spaces that are wheelchair accessible. The Giardini Pubblici, a large public garden, and the Sant'Elena Park are pleasant spots to relax and enjoy the outdoors. Additionally, the city's larger squares, such as Piazza San Marco, are relatively flat and more manageable.

If you're planning to visit museums, many have made improvements to ensure they are accessible. The Peggy Guggenheim Collection, for example, is known for its accessibility and offers support for visitors with disabilities. It's best to call ahead to inquire about specific facilities or services they offer.

Getting around the city can be easier with the help of accessibility guides and apps designed to assist travelers with disabilities. These resources provide valuable information on accessible routes, facilities, and services in Venice.

Overall, while Venice's unique layout poses some challenges, the city is making efforts to improve accessibility. With some preparation and by taking advantage of available

resources, you can enjoy a fulfilling and memorable visit. Be proactive about planning and don't hesitate to ask for assistance when needed. The city's charm and beauty are well worth the effort, and many visitors with disabilities find Venice to be a rewarding destination.

Sustainable Travel in Venice

Sustainable travel is becoming increasingly important, especially in a beautiful and historically rich city like Venice. As a traveler, there are several simple yet impactful ways you can help preserve the city's charm and minimize your environmental footprint.

First, consider how you get to Venice. If possible, choose train travel over flying. Trains produce less carbon dioxide and offer a scenic route into the city, which can be a pleasant start to your trip. Once in Venice, opt for walking or using public transportation like the Vaporetto (water bus) instead of taxis or car rentals. Venice's compact size makes it perfect for exploring on foot, and walking allows you to experience the city's unique details up close.

When using public transportation, look for eco-friendly options. The Vaporetto system has been working on reducing its environmental impact, so it's a good choice for getting around the city. Be mindful of waste while on board and dispose of your trash properly.

In terms of accommodation, choose hotels and lodgings that prioritize sustainable practices. Many hotels in Venice are adopting green initiatives, such as reducing energy consumption, minimizing waste, and using eco-friendly products. Look for certifications or inquire about their sustainability practices when booking your stay.

Dining sustainably is another key aspect. Venice offers a range of restaurants that focus on local and seasonal produce. By dining at these places, you support local farmers and reduce the carbon footprint associated with importing food. Many restaurants also offer vegetarian and vegan options, which generally have a lower environmental impact compared to meat-based dishes. Avoid single-use plastics and consider carrying a reusable water bottle to refill instead of buying bottled water.

Another way to contribute to sustainability is by supporting local businesses. Purchase souvenirs from local artisans rather than mass-produced items. This helps sustain traditional crafts and reduces the environmental impact associated with large-scale manufacturing and shipping.

When visiting attractions and historical sites, follow guidelines and respect the environment. Venice is facing challenges with tourism-related damage, so it's important to be considerate. Stick to marked paths to avoid damaging plants and structures, and follow any rules set by the sites you visit.

Participating in local clean-up efforts or eco-tourism activities can also make a difference. Some organizations in Venice offer tours and activities that include environmental education or contribute to local conservation efforts. Engaging in these activities can enhance your travel experience while benefiting the city.

Be aware of your overall consumption and try to reduce waste. Carry a reusable bag for shopping, use digital tickets when possible, and be conscious of your energy and water usage in accommodations. Small changes in your daily habits can add up to significant environmental benefits.

In summary, sustainable travel in Venice involves being mindful of your transportation choices, supporting eco-friendly businesses, reducing waste, and respecting the environment. By making these conscious decisions, you can enjoy your trip while helping to preserve the beauty and charm of Venice for future visitors.

CONCLUSION

As you prepare to embark on your journey to Venice, take a moment to reflect on what makes this destination so extraordinary. Venice is a place where the natural beauty of its canals and historic architecture converge to create a truly unique experience. The city offers a rich tapestry of outdoor adventures, from serene gondola rides to invigorating hikes in the nearby countryside. Its cultural heritage is woven into every corner, with stunning art, fascinating history, and a vibrant local culture waiting to be discovered. The culinary scene, with its tantalizing blend of traditional Venetian dishes and innovative flavors, is a feast for both the eyes and the palate.

My own connection to Venice is one of wonder and inspiration. I recall my first visit, where I wandered through the labyrinthine streets and discovered hidden squares that felt like they were straight out of a storybook. The way Venice can surprise you with its quiet charm and lively spirit makes it a place that continually inspires and delights. Whether it was savoring a perfectly prepared risotto or getting lost in the narrow alleys where local artisans work, each moment felt like a personal adventure.

I encourage you to embrace the Venice experience fully by stepping outside your comfort zone. Try a new activity that challenges you, such as navigating the city's maze of canals by gondola or sampling a local delicacy you've never encountered before. These experiences, though they might seem daunting, often lead to the most rewarding and memorable moments of your trip. The sense of accomplishment and discovery can transform your journey into a profound personal adventure.

Don't limit yourself to the well-trodden tourist paths. Venice has countless lesser-known spots and hidden gems that offer a glimpse into the city's true essence. Explore the quieter neighborhoods, visit local markets, and engage with the traditions and customs that define Venetian life. These off-the-beaten-path experiences can be incredibly enriching, often leading to serendipitous discoveries and unforgettable memories.

As you explore Venice, remember the importance of sustainable travel practices. Respect the environment by minimizing your ecological footprint, support local businesses, and engage in responsible tourism. Your efforts will help preserve the beauty and charm of Venice for future generations of travelers.

Before you set off, a few final tips can enhance your experience. Plan ahead but leave room for spontaneity; sometimes the best moments are unplanned. Engage with locals to gain insider recommendations and discover the city's hidden treasures. Being open to new experiences and interactions will enrich your journey.

I invite you to share your own stories and experiences from Venice. Whether through social media, travel blogs, or conversations with fellow travelers, your insights contribute to a vibrant community of explorers. Each story adds to the collective appreciation of this remarkable city.

As you embark on your adventure, remember that the beauty of travel lies in the exploration and the memories you create. Venice, with its timeless allure and rich experiences, offers a canvas for unforgettable moments. Embrace the journey, let the city's magic inspire you, and create your own cherished memories in this breathtaking region.

MAP
Scan QR Code with device to view map for easy navigation